Italian Operaismo

INSUBORDINATIONS / ITALIAN RADICAL THOUGHT
Lorenzo Chiesa, series editor

1. *The Monopoly of Man*, Anna Kuliscioff
2. *Convention and Materialism: Uniqueness without Aura*, Paolo Virno
3. *On Freud*, Elvio Fachinelli
4. *Italian Operaismo: Genealogy, History, Method*, Gigi Roggero

Italian Operaismo

Genealogy, History, Method

Gigi Roggero
translated by Clara Pope

The MIT Press / Cambridge, Massachusetts / London, England

© 2023 Massachusetts Institute of Technology

Originally published as *L'operaismo politico italiano. Genealogia, storia, metodo*
© 2019 DeriveApprodi

All rights reserved. No part of this book may be reproduced in any form by any electronic or mechanical means (including photocopying, recording, or information storage and retrieval) without permission in writing from the publisher.

This book was set in Arnhem Pro by New Best-set Typesetters Ltd. Printed and bound in the United States of America.

Library of Congress Cataloging-in-Publication Data is available.

ISBN: 978-0-262-04792-0

10 9 8 7 6 5 4 3 2 1

A barometric low hung over the Atlantic. It moved eastward toward a high-pressure area over Russia without as yet showing any inclination to bypass this high in a northerly direction. The isotherms and isotheres were functioning as they should. The air temperature was appropriate relative to the annual mean temperature and to the aperiodic monthly fluctuations of the temperature. The rising and setting of the sun, the moon, the phases of the moon, of Venus, of the rings of Saturn, and many other significant phenomena were all in accordance with the forecasts in the astronomical yearbooks. The water vapor in the air was at its maximal state of tension, while the humidity was minimal. In a word that characterizes the facts fairly accurately, even if it is a bit old-fashioned: It was a fine day in August 1913.
—Robert Musil, *The Man without Qualities*

Contents

Series Foreword / **ix**
Preface to the English Language Edition / **xiii**

1 **Context and Specificity: The Breeding Ground of Italian Political Operaismo** / 1
2 **From *Quaderni rossi* to Piazza Statuto** / 21
3 **The Trajectory of *Classe operaia*** / 45
4 **Operaismo beyond Operaismo** / 71
5 **A Dog in a Church: Romano Alquati by Guido Borio** / 95
6 **Returning to First Principles** / 127
  Appendix: Beyond Operaismo and So-Called Post-Operaismo / 159

Notes / **187**
Bibliography / **201**

Series Foreword

Insubordinations are creative and innovative double negations. They occur when an existing negative condition, the state of being "sub" or "under" a given order and thereby having an inferior rank, is countered by negating this very subjection. In our current late-capitalist predicament such a reversal acquires a more complex meaning. The ordering authority is in fact no longer simply in crisis and exposed to resistance but profoundly disordered in its own operative structure. Today, powers traditionally devoted to regulation perpetuate and reinforce their effectiveness by continually deregulating themselves. Orders become more and more oppressive precisely as they unveil the inconsistency on which they rest. As Pier Paolo Pasolini presciently put it almost fifty years ago, by now, "nothing is more anarchic than power." In this desolate scenario, actual insubordination cannot but arise as the tentative search for a *new* kind of order. Its long-term and admittedly ambitious mission is the establishment of a society without subordinates, called "communism." Its first and more realistic task is a taxonomic critique of an Order that resolves itself into myriad conflicting, yet no less tyrannical, suborders.

The present series aims to dissect the contemporary variant of the double negation involved in insubordination through the privileged prism of Italian radical thought. Starting from the late 1970s, Italy emerged as a laboratory for test-piloting the administration of the state of exception we are now living on a planetary level, both geopolitically and in our everyday lives. A brutal repression put an abrupt end to an intense season of social and political emancipations. But the theoretical elaboration of that defeat, which should not be confused with a grieving process, has managed to promote Italian radical thought to the center of a series of international debates that endeavor to define a new function and field of revolutionary politics. The series moves from the assumption that while so-called Italian Theory remains a vague and awkward category and attempts at hegemonizing it run the risk of resurrecting the idea of a national philosophy, it is beyond doubt that a growing number of left-wing Italian authors have, for good reasons, become very popular worldwide.

Drawing on philosophy, political theory, psychoanalysis, architecture, art history, anthropology, sociology, economics, and other fields, this interdisciplinary series intends to both further investigate consolidated Italian theories of emancipation and introduce authors (both present and past) who still remain largely unknown among Anglophone readers. Insubordinations: Radical Italian Thought will also foster original critical readings that pinpoint the tensions inherent to the oeuvre of prominent progressive thinkers and develop novel dialogues with various strands of post–World War II militant thought (such as heterodox Marxism, biopolitical theory, feminism of difference, social psychoanalysis, anti-psychiatry, and theories of Fascism). The series will also translate works by seminal earlier Italian authors who may be regarded as "forerunners" or critics *avant la lettre* of current trends in Italian radical thought.

It is my hope that, by delving into the titles of this series, readers will be able to appreciate the disciplined indiscipline they all share.

Lorenzo Chiesa

Preface to the English Language Edition

This book brings together six seminars on operaismo held between January and February 2019 at *Mediateca Gateway*, a library and center of political and militant formation in Bologna, Italy, which has now become *.input*. They are followed by the appendix, which consists of an interview laying out some of the problems facing us today. The title of the course, *Futuro anteriore*, was taken from a book published by DeriveApprodi in 2002, the result of a project of coresearch whose point of reference was Romano Alquati, which includes roughly sixty interviews with people connected to operaismo. The subtitle of that book, *Dai "Quaderni rossi" ai movimenti globali: Ricchezze e limiti dell'operaismo italiano* (From "Quaderni rossi" to the global movements: The wealth and limits of Italian operaismo), anticipates the political method that will be used here.

Now, as then, tracing the history of operaismo doesn't mean celebrating an icon or fixing an orthodoxy. Despite its "ism," operaismo always refused ideology and any loyalty to sacred scriptures. This began with its radical rereading of Marx and Lenin against the Marxism and Leninism that was dominant in the social communist tradition, in both its Stalinist and so-called heretical versions. We will revisit that history, our history, to overturn it against the present: not to contemplate it but to set it alight. To appropriate its wealth, to fight against its limits, to transform it into a political weapon. Not because continuity is possible, but because for us discontinuity means assuming the operaist *point of view* of partisan collectivity on and against this world. We must reject both the exaltation of the new and nostalgia for the past, the desire for the "post-" or the "pre-," as they are two sides of the same coin.

The term "militant formation" (*formazione militante*) should be clarified to avoid misunderstanding. It has nothing to do with indoctrination, based on ideological transmission, or with education, based on the transmission of pre-established values. On the contrary, it is a process of constructing a point of view and a capacity for critical reasoning, of being able to continually call into question or subvert the knowledge being formed. For a revolutionary militant, the *point of view* is an indispensable premise and at the same time that which must be continuously fought for. When we no longer have it or search for it, as premise and as conquest, we stop being militants. Today we are faced with the problem that most political militants have stopped engaging in militant formation and critical reasoning. In periods like this, then, in which we are unable to glimpse any possibility of radical transformation on the surface, there is a widespread tendency to flee into ideology, or into the values of micro-communities, seen today in the "bubbles" of political activists both on social networks and in real life. This consolatory form perhaps allows us to endure the current reality, but certainly not to fight it. In fact, the closest ally of that reality is everything that allows it to be endured by those who could or would like to fight against it.

The people who participated in the course—about thirty comrades from different generations, although mostly young—did so not to imbibe the words of the sacred scriptures but to find tools for rethinking the present, to dive down into the obscure ambivalences that bubble beneath the surface. Their contributions and questions were decisive in the spiral construction of the course, whose discursive style we have chosen to maintain here. For the sake of the fluency of the text, they have not been transcribed as interventions, but are directly incorporated into its development.

This explains one of the two reasons why the first-person plural is used and not the singular: it was a collective process. The other reason is that a militant is always a collective individual; when you go back to thinking, and thinking of yourself, as an "I," you cease to be a militant. The process of militant formation reaches the point where the individual both speaks and is spoken of from the *point of view*, in the sense we have alluded to and will elaborate on: not as a dogma, but because the point of view guides the way we see every aspect of the world and situates us within and against it. In other words, the militant is always part of a collective process; their subjectivity is formed through struggle against the modern individual, the abstract egoistic and solitary subject of the liberal and democratic tradition.

Operaismo is our point of view, it is a *method* or a *style*, our *Weltanschauung*. It is an irreducibly partial point of view, an irreducibly conflictual point of view, in relation to both the world and ourselves. Because in order to fight the world in which we live we must at the same time and continuously fight the world that is embodied in us, that produces and reproduces our lives, our way of seeing, our subjectivity.

In the last twenty years or so there has been a rediscovery or, perhaps more accurately, a discovery of operaismo on the international level. Since the publication of Negri and Hardt's *Empire* and the diffusion of its categories and lexicon in university departments across the world—where it has taken on the label of "Italian Theory" or "post-operaismo"—that revolutionary and irreducibly partisan political thought has definitively left the Italian province. But, in the process, it has been watered down and deprived of what made it revolutionary and partisan. The global university is an extraordinary machine of depoliticization: you can say whatever you want, as long as nothing you say affects the relationships of domination. This form of freedom neutralizes the radicality of thought, rendering it compatible with and functional to the machine of accumulation: the problem is not the absence of freedom but the liberal form of freedom. Thus, for reasons that will be explained in the text, that prefix—the "post-"—has engulfed the noun, neutralizing the method.

But be careful. This book does not set out to explain the "true" operaismo. For revolutionary militants, truth is never something that needs to be explained, but is always something that must be fought for, just like the point of view. Everything that is needed to fight the current reality is "true," everything that isn't needed isn't "true." In this book, then, readers will find themselves confronted with the radicality of operaismo in the literal sense: that is, the ability to get to the root of things, to grasp it, to try to tear it out or overthrow it. And the root is not underground, as you might think, but actually at the top, in the central points and contradictions. This requires a posture that isn't in thrall to fashions or dragged into the ephemeral vortex of public opinion. It means criticizing what everyone else accepts, also on a conceptual level. And it means criticizing what is accepted not only in the mainstream but also and above all in activist communities.

To give one example among many, we might think of the term "intersectionality," which has become fashionable in these circles. Here class disappears as a central contradiction and as conflict, being reduced to an economic fact that becomes one of the many identities located on a horizontal line, an identity of fragments in which every individual or small group can feel recognized in the hierarchy of subalternity. These identities are potentially infinite, much like the market. The sum of these fragments is never recomposed, or rather is always recomposed by capital. And so, having gone out the door, the old Marxist economism reenters through the window of intersectional identities, together with various other "isms." This book will explain why the operaist concept of class composition already anticipates by many decades the best critiques of intersectionality, insofar as gender and race dynamically and continually redetermine that composition. From the political point of view, class is composed through struggle and conflict, not on the basis of objective identities. It is not the exploited and the subaltern who compose themselves as a class, but those who struggle against their exploitation and subalternity. As Mario Tronti says: there is no class without class struggle. In the same way, the critique of universalism and historicism that has been so fashionable since the 1980s was practiced and anticipated by operaismo in a completely different direction, beginning from the irreducibility of the partisan point of view, and not—as was the case in the era of capitalist counterrevolution—from the end of the grand narratives with which the lexicon of the "post-" has endorsed the prohibition of the very conceivability of revolution. And the revolution means civil war, that is to say, the class struggle at the highest level of intensity. The operaist *polemos* is always the strong thought of subversion, never the weak thought of cultural and political relativism.

In short, the reader will find no room here for liberal pluralism, in which everyone can get together in the name of the general interest—including the general interests of community micro-identities. Because the general interest is always the interest of capital, and when everything is held together, it belongs to the bosses. On the contrary, the operaist method is, first and foremost, *divisive*. One side against the other; either you're on one side or you're on the other. And because of its formative character, this text will not give the reader ready-made answers or easy solutions; there will be no peace and quiet. Operaist formation uproots acquired convictions to get to the heart of the problem, for it is there, in that heart, that we must collectively and continuously reconstruct our capacity to *be against*. This is an act of force, of violence, that tears us away from the quiet management of our existence. Only those who are willing to be disturbed by this problem can open up the possibility of solving it.

Thus, the invitation we make to our readers is—as Alquati, one of our "tutelary deities," used to repeat continually—to use this book like a machine, not passively, but by acting to make it come alive, that is, as a tool that can be transformed to abolish the present state of things.

Gigi Roggero

1 Context and Specificity: The Breeding Ground of Italian Political Operaismo

In this and the following chapters we will raise issues, pose problems, and ask questions to which we will keep returning, moving forward not in a straight line but in a spiral. Rather than providing a bibliography in advance, recommendations for further reading will be given as we respond to the issues raised. The books, essays, and articles cited will not be exhaustive by any means, but will be partial references and summaries, providing starting points from which to dig deeper or move outward. This will be a collective process: on the one hand, because the book is taken from a course of seminars in which knowledge was not simply transmitted, but was constructed collectively; on the other hand, because what is written here is part of a collective history and a process of political cooperation.

Let's begin by asking, "Why operaismo?" It might seem counterintuitive to talk about operaismo when the subject at its base—the working class in the factory—

was defeated long ago or has at least lost its political centrality.

A brief aside: becoming politically central is a qualitative rather than a quantitative process. Despite the fact that the number of people working in factories across the world has increased, they are not politically central, or at least not in the same way as the factory working class that was the social and political reference of 1960s operaismo. People working in factories today behave very differently; their subjectivity is completely different: just because there are a lot of them doesn't mean we can call them a working class. When reading this book, keep in mind these concepts of quality and centrality, which are decisive for understanding the categories of class composition and subjectivity, as well as these questions: What do we mean by *operaietà*? In other words, what is the subjectivity of the figure around which the working class is politically recomposed? And does a new *operaietà* exist, or could it exist after the political collapse of the working class in the factory?

We can say from the start that operaismo is unfashionable or, to use a Nietzschean term to which we will return, "untimely."

Our next question is whether operaismo had anything to do with the glorification of factory workers as factory workers. We should first point out that other workerisms existed during the 1900s, and we will briefly summarize the main examples.[1]

First, there was councilism, which was at its strongest in the 1910s and 1920s and was based in the experiences of workers' councils or soviets. Some concrete examples include Rabociaia Oppositzia (Workers' Opposition) in the Soviet Union, whose most significant leaders were Alexandra Kollontai and Alexander Shliapnikov; Ordine Nuovo in Italy, centered in Turin, which included Antonio Gramsci; the German groups linked to the insurrection of the workers' councils at the end of the First World War;[2] and, among many other militant thinkers, the Dutch theorist Anton Pannekoek.

The central figure in the councilist movement was the *craft worker* (*operaio di mestiere*), considered to be better than the bosses at running the factory. This leads to a vision of the self-management of the factory and society by workers united in the collective form of the council. Thus councilism involves the glorification of the figure of the worker as such, a work ethic that isn't simply ideology but is rooted in a specific class composition, in which this worker and their pride in their craft plays an important role in the productive process. These workers bear the stamp of their predecessors, the artisans. They are a sort of split artisan, struggling to regain complete autonomy over their skills, capacities, and forms of organization. Councilism fights against the expropriation of the crafts, which is implicit in industrial development, and tries to guide development toward a strengthening of the collective autonomy of the working class. To simplify, we could say that the councilist movement's perspective on self-management doesn't deny the tactical function of the party, but forcefully asserts the strategic hegemony of the soviet.

Lenin's critiques of councilism are relatively well-known. His text *"Left Wing" Communism: An Infantile Disorder*, which is now more often cited than read, was used in the decades that followed by various communist parties (including the Italian Communist Party) as an argument against all forms of class autonomy. We would instead recommend reading the debate on the function of trade unions in the Soviet Union between 1920 and 1921, a few years after the Bolsheviks took power; and three lectures held in 1967 in Montreal by the Black communist C. L. R. James, which were dedicated to this subject.[3] We will now briefly summarize that debate. On the one hand, Lenin argued against Trotsky and Bukharin, who, coming from a bureaucratic perspective, wanted a complete statalization or even militarization of the trade unions, reducing them to a means for transmitting Soviet power. On the other hand, he heavily criticized Workers' Opposition for their naive democratic ideology: it was as if they thought that workers' control was a natural point of departure rather than a process to fight for. We would say, perhaps forcing the argument a little, that the questions of workers' autonomy and the extinction of the state are central to the debate on the function of the trade union. Trotsky and Bukharin denied them;

Workers' Opposition hoped for them as if it were simply a question of ideological will. But for Lenin they were important strategic stakes in the struggle, the fruit of a political process made up of conflict, organization, and the overturning of the relations of force. In this sense, it was precisely in that particular historical period that the trade union was not what it had been before and was not destined to be what it would later become: it would have to be used tactically, as a school for class struggle and for the development of workers' autonomy, toward the extinction of the state.

Also at stake in this debate was the relationship between the soviet and the party, or rather, the old question of spontaneity versus organization. For Lenin, it was indeed a *relationship*, and so never given once and for all. This can be seen in his continually changing point of view between 1905 and 1917: there are periods in which spontaneity is more advanced—as happens with the revolutionary process after the Bloody Sunday of January 1905 and with the soviets between February and July of 1917. In these cases organization had to follow spontaneity, rethink it, and reform it by beginning from it. There were other periods, such as between July and October 1917, when the party had to reinvigorate the soviets, who were at risk of falling into a stagnant democratic parliamentarism. In these cases organization was used to reopen the way for the full development of spontaneity.[4]

In addition to councilism, there was another workerism of a very different, or even opposite, kind: the Stalinist workerism of the 1930s. In this case it was not the soviets that were central, but the party.[5] However, the working class played an important role, being used against the intellectual and peasant petit bourgeoisie. Although it was a symbolic and instrumental reference, it produced concrete effects, both in terms of workers' participation in the managing bodies of the party and, most importantly, in the exchange between obedience to the regime and relative technical autonomy. Rita di Leo describes it as something like a pact between the party-state and the workers, which guaranteed power to the former and a certain role in managing the pace of work to the latter, in apparent contradiction with the Stakhanov myth. But the contradiction is relative: the slow pace of production in the Soviet factories, which would continue in the following decades, was in fact a concession made in exchange for the symbolic role that the working class played in Soviet ideology—glorifying the proletarian condition and labor as something to be extended, not abolished.

Unlike Marx, who saw being a productive worker not as a blessing but as a misfortune, the Marxist and social communist tradition saw it not as a misfortune but as a blessing, and one that should be generalized across the whole of society: the bright future was to be painted in the gloomy colors of labor and exploitation.

After this long but necessary premise, we approach the theme of our chapter: context and specificity. Let's begin from the context: Italy in the 1950s was a political desert, in which any genuine revolutionary perspective had been abandoned. The partisan resistance to fascism had become an icon: the mythicization of that experience was directly proportional to its depoliticization. The iconization of the Resistance in the popular imagination helped the Communist Party to put an end to it in the reality of the class, in the same way as Napoleon's celebration of the French Revolution was the final nail in its coffin. The more that something is sanctified as heavenly, the more difficult it is to repeat it on earth.

The political desert of that period was visible in the factories. In 1955, the Communist Party–affiliated Italian Federation of Metalworkers (Fiom)[6] was defeated in the elections for FIAT's Internal Commission, which represented the workers' trade unions in the factory. It was both a shock to the Italian Communist Party (PCI) and seen as a confirmation of its long-held and mistaken realism, in which the working class was considered to have lost all revolutionary potential. This led the party in a new direction: the pursuit of the middle classes and the "Italian road to socialism," which in the 1970s would become the search for the "historic compromise." This created a vicious circle: the leaders of the PCI, who held that the working class was finished, asked the communist and unionist cadre what was going on in the factories, who told them that nothing was happening, which just confirmed what they already thought at the top, further reinforcing their strategy. The PCI's position, which had been built around its own interests, was a sort of Frankfurtism before its time. It wouldn't be long before it was widely accepted that the Western working class had inevitably become integrated into capitalism's iron cage. What's more, at that time, not even sociology, which in Italy was still pretty insignificant, was interested in the factory (with a few exceptions, including the work of Alessandro Pizzorno on the experience of Olivetti in Ivrea[7]).

However, from the point of view of the relations of production and organization of work in Italy, the 1950s were particularly significant. Lagging behind other Western countries such as the United States and Germany, it was only in this period that Italy experienced the full development of Taylorism-Fordism. Let's briefly clarify what these often-misunderstood terms mean, as they will come in useful when we get closer to the present and discuss the passage to so-called post-Fordism.

Taylorism is a system for the scientific organization of factory work marked by mass and serial production, the planning of time and rhythms, and the maximizing of worker functionality to the system of machines. It is the regime of the production line, of the stopwatch, and of the alienation of the worker, who is tendentially reduced to an appendix of the machine. It is the hollowing-out of the craft of the worker on which the councilist movement had been built: workers' skills are expropriated and incorporated into machines, craftsmanship is progressively destroyed, and any pride in work disappears in its alienating repetitiveness. Taylor's dream was to one day put monkeys to work on the production line. It remained a dream. The scientific organization of labor would never work according to the engineer's abstract project.[8]

The first place in which the Taylorist regime was applied was the large-scale production of the Ford factory. In the 1910s, Ford had an idea that would later become hegemonic: by increasing the salaries of the workers, a virtuous circle would be activated between production and consumption. In January 1914, the minimum wage was doubled from $2.38 to $5 an hour. For the first time, the workers could afford some of the cars that they produced. As Ford is meant to have said: "Americans can have any kind of car they want, and any color they want, as long as it's a Ford, and as long as it's black." A series of apparent "benefits" for the workers was added to that, from houses to recreational areas. This initiative was driven not by the philanthropy of bosses, as they tried and still try to make us believe, but by an attempt to optimize the regime of labor, "industrial welfare," and exploitation, as well as by the need to respond to the powerful struggles of the American working class.

To summarize: Taylorism is a model for the organization of factory labor, Fordism is a model for the organization of workers in society. Taylorism-Fordism mapped out the coordinates of the factory and society in which workers lived and were exploited, which would be further developed in the welfare state politics of the following decades.

We must keep this bigger picture in mind in order to avoid falling into the idea that there was an inevitability to the birth and development of Italian political operaismo. Not only was there nothing that allowed it to be predicted, but it was also in some sense "untimely." We come back to this word, whose Nietzschean use we hinted at before: untimeliness is acting against time, on time, and for a time that is to come. Not outside time, but *within and against* time. Not an idealist action but a materialist one. There is no trace of utopia, of yearning for another possible world: it instead echoes Lenin's "We should dream!" in *What Is to Be Done?*, refusing to accept the time we are given, in order to instead construct our own time, an autonomous time, produced through struggle and opposition.

For the Italian communists the 1950s were also marked by international events, *in primis* their relationship with the Soviet Union. The most important include the 1953 workers' revolt in East Berlin, the Hungarian insurrection between October and November 1956, and, in February of the same year, the Twentieth Congress of the Communist Party of the Soviet Union, in which Stalinism and its cult of personality were denounced.

This was heartbreaking for the Italian communists. But their formal de-Stalinization did not correspond to a real de-Stalinization, and the tanks in Budapest were a reminder of that: the PCI wholeheartedly defended them, despite the trauma felt at its base. Some militants saw more possibilities for action within the Italian Socialist Party (PSI). Raniero Panzieri, a founding figure of *Quaderni rossi*, started out in the latter. Others moved to the PSI as exiles from the PCI, such as Alberto Asor Rosa in Rome, or from other groups, like Toni Negri in Veneto, who had started out with the young Catholics in FUCI (the Italian Catholic Federation of University Students).

However, in this period an antagonist and revolutionary political initiative that went beyond the institutions of the workers' movement was pretty hard to imagine. So much so that, in the following decade, the comrades of *Quaderni rossi* and *Classe operaia* were often verbally and even physically attacked when they went to factory gates without the mediation of the party or the union, addressing their leaflets directly to the workers.

Obviously, the old minorities still existed, in particular the Bordigist and Trotskyist groups, characterized by their heavy critique of the course taken by the Communist Party, and ennobled by their opposition to Stalinism. These included militants who would later become important for operaismo, such as the Bordigist Danilo Montaldi from Cremona, the French Trotskyist journal *Socialisme ou barbarie*, and the already cited

C. L. R. James, who also came from Trotskyism. These groups should be interpreted as symptoms of the fact that the communist movement was not entirely pacified. However, these communist "heresies"—save for a few heterodox exceptions such as those we have just mentioned—often ended up restoring Marxist dogmas rather than calling them into question. The critique of Stalin turned into a critique of anyone who strayed from the objective tracks of History,[9] and thus into an attack on subjectivism in the name of a traditional determinism. This was more or less the destiny and essence of these heresies, denouncing those who deviated from the straight and narrow, aiming to return to the authority of the sacred scripts.

We can find other symptoms of a critique of orthodox Marxism in this period, which are even more important for us because they make up a significant part of the breeding ground for that subjectivity that gave rise to Italian political operaismo. For example, Galvano Della Volpe—a thinker initially formed in the tradition of Gentile's idealism who then explicitly broke with him—taught in the faculty of literature and philosophy in Rome and had a strong influence on Mario Tronti, Alberto Asor Rosa, Gaspare de Caro, and Umberto Coldagelli, all of whom would later contribute to *Quaderni rossi* and *Classe operaia*.

In 1946 Della Volpe published *La libertà comunista*, in which he grappled with the relation between freedom and communism. As Tronti wrote in his rereading of the text in 2000, the problem that Della Volpe posed is the "contact-conflict between liberty and communism. Not between liberalism and socialism. Direct contact and conflict between the problem of liberty and the perspective of communism."[10] Communist freedom is a rupture with liberal freedom; it is thus no surprise that, in the following years, the targets of Della Volpe's critique were the liberal scholar Norberto Bobbio and the Italian communist leader Palmiro Togliatti, who had tried to weaken the opposition between freedom and communism by adapting the PCI to the liberal democratic regime. This was an example of Togliatti's ambiguity, respecting democratic institutions while professing loyalty to the revolution. But, in fact, by tactically presenting himself as democratic and liberal, revolutionary strategy was left behind. Della Volpe's Marxism was materialist and antihistoricist, theorizing a rupture and not a continuity between Hegel and Marx. His was a Marxism in extreme tension with the history of Marxism, an attempt to begin again from Marx that came very close to rethinking him from scratch. It was no longer strictly Marxist, although perhaps it was not yet Marxian; operaismo would take up that baton.

Another important figure is the previously cited Danilo Montaldi. Breaking with its Togliattian politics, he left the PCI and took on a more internationalist Bordigist position. He collaborated with some important journals in the 1950s, including *Discussioni*, *Nuovi argomenti*, *Ragionamenti*, *Opinione*, and *Passato e presente*, all of which played an important role in the circulation of debates and critical thought. In 1960 he published *Milano, Corea*, with Franco Alasia, an inquiry into immigrants in the suburbs of Milan; a year later *Autobiografie della leggera*; and in 1970, *Militanti politici di base*. Montaldi is the main point of reference for a particular type of participatory and militant inquiry aimed at activating the research subjects. Later we will look at its similarities with and differences from Alquatian coresearch, but for now we will simply say that he focused on those political and social figures who were gradually being pushed to the margins of the process of modernization and industrialization, which had developed rapidly in the Po Valley and in the area around Cremona where he lived and was politically active.

Montaldi also made a vital contribution through building a network of international contacts. It was he who had the strongest relationship with Socialisme ou Barbarie, a political group (also centered around a journal) that included Edgar Morin, Claude Lefort, Cornelius Castoriadis, and Daniel Mothé. The group had broken with the French Communist Party to create a Marxism that brought together different traditions (in addition to the abovementioned Trotskyism, there were clear influences from councilism, libertarianism, and workers' management). They aimed to reread Marx in a way that was critical of Marxism and to rethink the relationship between communism and freedom.

Aut aut, founded in 1951 by Enzo Paci, was another journal that engaged in many important discussions and debates. A philosopher who taught at the University of Pavia and then at the University of Milan, Paci's rethinking of Marx was influenced by his relationship with Husserlian phenomenology. A group of young students formed around him, including Guido Davide Neri, Enrico Filippini, Giovanni Piana, Pier Aldo Rovatti, and, later, Giairo Daghini. This group of phenomenologists set up the Commune of Via Sirtori in Milan, in which Romano Alquati, Pierluigi Gasparotto, and Sergio Bologna took part. The Commune became an international meeting point for political debate and discussion.

We could continue to follow the major and minor genealogies of what would later become operaismo (for example, citing the experience of Danilo Dolci in Sicily and his appeal to "go to the people," which was answered by several militants who would later become part of *Quaderni rossi* and *Classe operaia*, such as Mauro Gobbini and Negri).[11] But we will not do that here. We simply want to emphasize the character of the 1950s as a period of *transition*. However, we mustn't forget that it is only retrospectively that we are able to attribute a historicist and teleological character to that transition. In that period, on the surface we would have seen only dismay, chaos, and resignation. Reflecting on that together, we could say that the transition isn't sent to us by History but must be won by acting against History.

We should now focus on the crucial common element that brings the future operaist militants together: fighting a sense of defeat, seeking out strength, putting the problem of a revolutionary rupture back on the agenda. Their biographies tell specific and different stories: there were those who, like the Roman comrades, largely came from the Communist Party group in the university and were searching for a different point of view, either in explicit rupture with the party or in order to push the party toward revolutionary positions; there were those who, like the Venetians, came from heterogeneous groups, from social Catholicism or the Socialist Party, and gathered in the struggle at Porto Marghera amid the rampant industrialization of the Northeast; there were others who, in Lombardy and Piedmont, felt—as Alquati said—"humiliated and insulted, marginalized and bitter," as a result of their proletarianization or lumpen-proletarianization following the end of the Second World War. "This downfall was soon felt by me as ambivalent: as a great everyday tragedy, but also as a further liberation."[12]

Even in their differences (here summarized in an extremely cursory way), these biographies demonstrate a rupture with the cult of victimhood that had always been a constitutive part of the Left and much of the social communist tradition. It was not passion for the oppressed that guided them, but the search for those who struggled against their conditions of oppression. It was not about laying low in resistance, but about building a plan for attack; not about pitying weakness but about identifying force. For the future operaist militants, this would also be a rupture with themselves, with their own subjectivities and personal histories. A rupture that opened the way to new encounters and new trajectories, to a history that would become collective.

In the apparent desert of the 1950s, that force could be the working class: that was the gamble, against everything and everyone, on which operaismo was founded. Not the working class as described in social communist iconography, which sacrificed itself for the general and universal interest, for the progress of humanity, for a brighter future. No, a specific working class that struggled in the alienation of the Taylorist factory, in the pacification of Fordist society, in their abandonment by the workers' movement institutions. A working class that didn't sacrifice itself for the general interest but that followed the irreducibility of its own partial interest, a working class that wasn't dazzled by the promise of progress and a better future but that wanted everything and straight away, a working class that didn't take pride in its work but that refused it. Not the weak, docile working class, with bowed heads, whom the Left liked so much. In fact, they had more in common with the workers depicted by Ernst Jünger, an important conservative thinker of the 1900s and an exceptional writer who volunteered in the First World War and was awarded the Iron Cross, who then became a Nazi and an officer in the Wehrmacht, although later turned against Hitler. If you want to understand what the mass worker is in essence, its possible collective form, potentially powerful and concretely ambiguous, read *Storm of Steel*, his diary of the First World War, or *The Worker*, an incendiary antibourgeois manifesto. You will then begin to understand what Tronti meant when he said that a great reactionary is better than a small revolutionary.

So, against the plethora of small revolutionaries of the 1950s, this heterogenous group found themselves having to start again from nothing: starting again from Marx against Marxism, from Lenin against Leninism. Not to claim the objectivity of the Word, as the various heresies had done, but to practice the subjectivity of conflict. They took an untimely gamble on a working class that didn't want to be humiliated and insulted, abandoned, defeated, and given up for dead. And they created a workerism of a new kind, in rupture with its predecessors on at least one fundamental point: it was a workerism against work, a workerism that struggled not for the extension of the workers' condition but, on the contrary, for its abolition. A workerism that didn't glorify the workers as such but was searching for workers who acted against themselves, against their own conditions of exploitation and their subjectivity as formed by capital. (Today's glorification of calloused hands and greasy overalls has nothing to do with Italian political operaismo.) Operaismo didn't look back at what no longer existed, at the myths of the Resistance and at the sacred icons of the workers' movement, but searched for that which didn't exist but could exist; it tried to identify and organize the mole that dug where nobody thought it was possible to dig, and whose tracks, invisible on the surface, actually seemed to point in the opposite direction.

When, in 1960, the electro-mechanical workers in Milan and Genoa went on strike, the so-called striped T-shirts burst onto the scene,[13] and the initial gamble of the operaisti began to take form. Two years later, the riot of Piazza Statuto baptized the mass worker as a central figure in the class struggle.[14] But we must remember that things always seem to add up in retrospect: the 1950s as the prelude to the 1960s, the passage to Taylorism-Fordism as the terrain for the incubation of the mass worker, the calm before the storm. The point, however, is that there is nothing necessary in any of this. In politics there is no hindsight. And, politically, it is precisely in those periods when it seems that nothing is happening that the capacity to anticipate must be put into action and the revolutionary gamble must be taken. Because when it's already happening, you are too late.

This is one of the first lessons that we learn from the history of operaismo, of which this chapter has traced the genealogy. A history against the Left, in rupture with Marxism and the social communist tradition. A history, we should clarify, that ended with the decline of the figure on which it was built: the mass worker. So why still talk about it? Because in the bowels of this history we can find the method, the timely or untimely style, of the operaist point of view.

2 From *Quaderni rossi* to Piazza Statuto

In the first chapter we loosely mapped out the terrain in which Italian political operaismo would take root: the urgent need to return to Marx against Marxism, to break the sense of defeat and the victimist culture of the Left and much of the social communist tradition, to search for strength rather than weakness.

We could describe this terrain as analogous to the medium in which bacteria are cultured, drawing on a metaphor used by Churchill when describing October 1917: "They turned upon Russia the most grisly of weapons. They transported Lenin in a sealed truck like a plague bacillus from Switzerland to Russia." This term, "plague bacillus," encapsulates operaist militants and political militants in general, who root themselves in an enemy body, struggle against it, and try to destroy it. They don't arise randomly, but only from a medium. Yet there is no predetermined trajectory from the existence of a medium to the development of bacteria. There is no necessity, just possibility, and many things are needed to realize that possibility. Not simply the Machiavellian categories of virtue and fortune, but also the development of subjectivity. This process can thus go in different or even opposite directions. Here we can already see glimpses of a *materialism of possibility* rather than of necessity. We will now start to lay the bases for a discourse on tendency that rescues it from teleology and historicism.

In the previous chapter we talked about being within and against time. Those who later became operaist militants broke with Marxism and with that which had become the communist movement, and also broke with themselves. This is both a specific experience and a general truth: revolutionary militants are always located within and against the time in which they live; they thus have to begin from a rupture with themselves, with their own conditions, ways of thinking, forms of life, and relationships. Revolutionary militants are those who have the courage to repeatedly break with the present. When they lose that courage, they stop being revolutionary militants.

Beginning from these ruptures and common problems, from a sense of dissatisfaction with the given answers and an instinctive movement toward new questions, the different subjects in this heterogenous medium came together to form a new journal, *Quaderni rossi*. Individual histories stopped being individual, interweaving in a collective history.

Raniero Panzieri was a central figure in the founding of the journal. Born in 1921, he was older than the others and had taken part in land occupations in Sicily toward the end of the 1940s. As we've seen, many at this time saw the socialist party as providing a more open and independent space within the workers' movement institutions. We've mentioned Asor Rosa, who had left the PCI, and Negri, who had come from the young Catholics. There were also others at the peripheries of operaist history, such as the sociologist Roberto Giducci, who was close to the Olivettian "community"; Gianni Bosio, with his focus on working and living conditions and popular culture (we should mention the journal *Nuovo canzoniere italiano* [New Italian songbook]); and Franco Fortini, a poet, literary critic, and militant who was involved in a number of journals, including *Quaderni piacentini*. Panzieri was particularly important in the socialist party at that time, joining its central committee in 1953 and becoming its culture secretary a year later. In 1957 he coedited *Mondo operaio* and in February 1958 wrote the article "Sette tesi sul controllo operaio" (Seven theses on workers' control) with Lucio Libertini, which was published in the journal's second issue. There are clear echoes of councilism in its arguments for direct political action and a rank-and-file workers' democracy.

Panzieri was a critic of the party form, in particular that which he claimed was its nefarious identity with class, seeing this as the source of the Stalinism dominant in the PCI. In opposition to this he stressed class autonomy and the need to start again from the economic struggle within the factories of neo-capitalism (which was actually no longer "new" and was even in decline in other parts of the Western world). He pointed to the gap between the institutions of the workers' movement (the party and the trade union) and the real movement of the class, arguing that this problem should be the starting point for rethinking political action, an argument that would later be developed in *Quaderni rossi*. He also criticized the relationship between communist intellectuals and the party, in particular arguing against the ideal of the organic intellectual, a figure that had become a simple cultural administrator in the service of the organization. From this perspective, Panzieri deepened his analysis of neo-capitalism, most famously in "Sull'uso capitalistico delle macchine" (On the capitalist use of machines), which was published in the first issue of *Quaderni rossi*. He explained that technology and machines were permeated by social relations: their development was not driven by the aim of increasing the forces of production, as Marxist determinism would have it, but was instead shaped by class struggle. Panzieri focused on the factory as the place in which struggles could break out. He thus sought to prioritize a dialogue with the trade unions, something that characterized *Quaderni rossi* from the outset. But he was skeptical about whether these struggles could be generalized across the whole of society.

At the end of the 1950s, Panzieri moved to Turin in Piedmont, where he worked for the publishing house Einaudi. A group of young sociologists formed around him, including Vittorio Rieser, Giovanni Mottura, Dario and Liliana Lanzardo, and Bianca Beccalli. Marxism had traditionally either ignored or despised sociology as a bourgeois mystification. After all, what was the point of looking to the social sciences if Marxism already explained everything there was to know about capitalist society? Instead, *Quaderni rossi* started calling into question not sociology itself, but its *bourgeois use*, with the aim of reformulating workers' inquiry.

Others, most notably, Romano Alquati, proposed a different use of sociology. He chose a path that was complementary to that of Danilo Montaldi, who, like Alquati, was also from Cremona: rather than looking for subjects who were marginalized from the process of capitalist industrial modernization as Montaldi did, Alquati sought out those at its center—a center not only of exploitation but also of possibilities for conflict. He hypothesized that it was a site of ambivalence and wagered on the potential for refusal and struggle inherent in its emergent subjectivity. In search of this center, he moved first to Milan and then to Turin, where he stayed for the rest of his life.

In Milan he met the group of phenomenologists and the Commune of Via Sirtori, becoming particularly close to one of Paci's students, Guido Davide Neri. There he also met Pierluigi Gasparotto, moving with him to the factory-city of Turin. Already in the 1950s, Alquati was focusing on how Italy's belated development might make it possible to anticipate the tendency. So, paying particular attention to places in which Taylorism-Fordism and the worker linked to it had already fully developed, he studied American industrial sociology and French sociology of labor, and read texts on economics, anthropology, and the science of organization, as well as history and philosophy. This contributed to the construction of the practice of coresearch. He discovered that the presumed objectivity of the scientific organization of labor was a mystification in the properly Marxist sense, concealing the social relations and conflict that underlaid and shaped it. The Taylorist factory didn't actually ever work according to Taylor's abstract scheme, but instead functioned through the continual valorization of the multiple forms of resistance carried out by workers in order to save their labor power and free up time. Struggle and even sabotage, if they didn't reach an irreversible point of rupture, could be captured and recuperated, transformed and put to work within the cogs of capitalist valorization and reorganization. The bosses' machine was fed by stealing workers' knowledge. Here we see the forceful return of the Marx of *The*

Poverty of Philosophy, who explained that the biggest productive force of capital was the revolutionary working class. But it returns in a new way, in the heart of capitalist development, as part of an unprecedented antagonism between the mass worker and the Taylorist factory. Tronti's later reversal is already at work here: the first principle is working-class struggle; capitalist development is the response and not the premise. Thus his call to "change orientation"[1] can already be seen here in embryonic form.

As we spiral forward, let's take up again the questions of temporality and of the *tendency*, a concept that is as central as it is ambiguous in the history of Italian political operaismo. First, the tendency is primarily that of workers' subjectivity, of their formation into a class, of their behaviors and forms of expression, and only as a result of that is it the tendency of capitalist development. Or rather, it is the tendency of the capitalist social relationship, and so of class antagonism. Second, the tendency is not linear, chronological, and deterministic. The fact that Italy was lagging behind other parts of the world provided the opportunity for anticipation, but this doesn't mean that everything always develops in the same way; on the contrary, it is precisely because things don't develop in the same way that the identification of how things have gone enables us to act on the tendency, to deviate it, to overturn it, to break it. The tendency is therefore a field of possibility that is materially founded, whose direction depends on class struggle and on the force of an organized subjectivity.

In their efforts to anticipate subjective tendencies, Alquati and others made use of workers' diaries, themselves extraordinary examples of inquiry. Of particular importance was *Journal d'un ouvrier (1956–1958)* by Daniel Mothé, who was a militant in the Renault factory in France and, as noted, was active in Socialisme ou Barbarie, as well as Paul Romano's *The American Worker*, translated into Italian by Montaldi and published in part in the Bordigist journal *Battaglia comunista* in the mid-1950s. To this we should add James Boggs's *The American Revolution: Pages from a Negro Worker's Notebook*. Boggs was a Black militant and worker at Chrysler in Detroit, and a member of the "Correspondence Publishing Committee"—initially together with C. L. R. James, but later going their separate ways when the group split. Although we are only cursorily mentioning these names and groups, they should help us to map out a sort of *operaist cartography* of the people, practices, and political paths that intertwined in a context that, while having a crucial specificity in Italy, had an international reach from the start.

The comrades in Rome were also pivotal to the foundation of *Quaderni rossi*. The members of the group, who all had links to the Italian Communist Party, first met at La Sapienza university, where they attended Galvano Della Volpe's lectures. They were later joined by the young Rita di Leo. In 1959, at only twenty-eight years old, Tronti had already confronted the idealistic tradition of Italian Marxism and even the untouchable Gramsci (a Gramsci who had been disembodied and "revised" by Togliatti, in order to make him functional to the PCI line—which is the very reason why he had become an untouchable icon). We see here the beginnings of Tronti's "Marxian purification of Marxism," which returned Marx to a workers' point of view within and against bourgeois society.[2]

In his essay on Gramsci, Tronti writes: "For Italian philosophy, Marx was a *foothold* for arriving at Hegel."[3] Croce and Gentile both said this explicitly, even if in different ways. This led Tronti to argue that, in Italy, rather than being confused with positivism, Marx had served to combat it. All truth, even that of Marx, had become concentrated in idealism: "Marx is thus at the origins of Italian idealism.... Conclusion: *we had a Hegel who was tendentially Marxian and a Marx who was tendentially Hegelian*."[4] The decisive factor, then, was not the liquidation of Marxism but its idealistic interpretation: "First you make all of Marx revolve around Hegel, then you cut Hegel out of the middle and say: look, Marx can't turn on his own. This is an example of the interpretation of a theory coinciding with its liquidation."[5] Here we see Tronti making the Della Volpean rupture we referred to in the previous chapter, emphasizing a break and not a continuity between Marx and Hegel.

After having critically retraced the entire tradition of Italian Marxism, Tronti returns to Gramsci, whom he already reckoned with at the beginning of his article. His thesis is that Gramsci is a typically and fundamentally Italian thinker, steeped in a coherently historicist conception of the real. And given that historicism is the truth of idealism, the official Italian Marxism of the 1950s turned out to be caught in a line of continuity going from De Sanctis to Gramsci via Croce. It is this line that had to be broken. While attacking Croce and Gentile, even presenting himself as anti-Croce, Gramsci ended up actually accepting the basis of their thought. Gramsci is therefore the antithesis of Hegel, not a rupture with him: a negation that allows for the dialectical affirmation of the positive rather than its destruction. In other words, the apparent deviation from the Hegel-Croce-Gentile line is actually its continuation: the idealistic and therefore speculative identification of history and philosophy is substituted with a historicist and thus fully real identification. To make a break with the idealist culture of the PCI, there needed to be a break with Gramsci himself, rather than simply with his Togliattian reworking.

We have now laid out the context: restless subjects moved by the desire for rupture, theoretical elaborations that substantiate hypotheses related to practice, and different histories that meet and give rise to a collective political experience. In other words, an encounter between conditions of possibility and expressions of will. This is the context in which *Quaderni rossi* is cultivated. Right from its first issue in 1961, different perspectives and various tensions were evident, which, although coming together for the short life of the journal, soon reached a breaking point. A number of trade unionists contributed to that issue. The opening article, "Lotte operaie nello sviluppo capitalistico" (Workers' struggles in capitalist development), was entrusted to Vittorio Foa, who had taken part in the Resistance, was a socialist and one of the leaders of Giuseppe Di Vittorio's CGIL at the end of the 1940s, and the National Secretary of Fiom in the fateful year of 1955 in which the union suffered electoral defeat in FIAT's Internal Commission. Sergio Garavini and Emilio Pugno, both of whom held leadership positions in Fiom and the PCI in Turin, were also involved at the beginning. The relationship between struggles and trade unions was central to that issue of *Quaderni rossi*. It was explored not only in Foa's editorial but in the sections "Esperienze e resoconti sindacali" (Union experiences and reports) and "Alcuni dati sulle lotte sindacali a Torino 1960–1961" (Some data on union struggles in Turin, 1960–1961). After all, from Panzieri's perspective, *Quaderni rossi* was a tool of critique and inquiry with which to create tensions within and transform the workers' movement institutions. But the relationship with the trade union leaders didn't last long, coming to an end after the first issue. The second issue included a text in which Franco Mogliano, a prominent figure in the Olivettian "community" in Ivrea, laid out his opposition to the arguments in *Quaderni rossi*, in particular in relation to their unsettling hypothesis of a nascent workers' autonomy.

We should note that, even for Alquati and those who would later set up *Classe operaia*, the rupture with the trade unions never meant indifference to the role that they played. On the contrary, they would prove useful for entering the factories, just as the relationship with the trade unionists remained a critical point in the development of struggles, to facilitate workers' autonomous communication and organization, or at least to avoid them going off in the wrong direction.

Quaderni rossi's center of gravity was the factory-city of Turin and its surroundings: the FIAT and Lancia factories, the network of smaller factories and industries in the provinces (from the RIV factory at Pinerolo to the cotton mills of the Susa Valley), and obviously Olivetti in Ivrea. They gambled on the idea that workers' struggles would begin again there, in the beating heart of Taylorization. But for Alquati this was not about restarting struggles in traditional terms, as if merely picking up a dropped thread, which was the hope of the most advanced and radical parts of the trade union. The wager was rather that these struggles would have a new worker at their center, that is, new behaviors and a new subjectivity, potentially breaking with the Taylorist factory and at the same time with the traditional institutions of the workers' movement. These were what Alquati would call the "new forces" available to the class struggle.

Already in the first issue of *Quaderni rossi* a political hypothesis had clearly emerged from the practice of coresearch; it can be found in Alquati's "Documenti sulla lotta di classe alla FIAT" (Documents on class struggle at FIAT) and his presentation on FIAT at the PSI congress in January 1961, which pointed to these "new forces." His empirical generalizations, he tells us, are obtained "without worrying too much about rigor in method, because its objective is to give rise to further work and hypotheses, with the distant aim of pushing for a movement that is solidly 'founded,' which alone would provide the conditions for a dynamic verification and generalization." For Alquati the desire to start again from scratch was the point of departure, assuming the end of a political phase: "From '54, in tandem with large investments in technological modernization, there was an offensive that eliminated from the factory a workers' movement that had already been defeated much earlier. In Turin this story had another generation as its protagonist, represented in the factory by the 'old people' (at FIAT you grow old fast). Today's protagonists are used to beginning their discourse from '56." In other words, you can't go back. The common traits of the newly emerging conflicts needed to be captured: "The workers' resurgence in Turin was not so much a consequence of the movement in Genoa, as one of the facts that contributed toward determining it." The common trait was therefore that of a new generation, a new force, a new subjectivity, with behaviors that no longer accepted reformist solutions and went far beyond any possibility of recuperation on the part of the traditional institutions of the workers' movement. Thus, unlike what Panzieri had thought, workers' struggles could become generalized on the social level. These "new forces" were not making themselves available to the party and the trade unions. On the contrary, if they wanted to survive, the party and trade unions had to make themselves available to these "new forces." After all, when faced with the struggles at FIAT, it was the militants who were members of Fiom and the PCI—in particular those of the older generation—who acted as an obstacle to strikes.

Alquati concluded his presentation to the PSI congress saying that "the situation of the new workers at FIAT seems in many ways widely generalizable."[6] He went on: "*Young people are not willing to join with strata or organisms that are foreign to the working class, for it is precisely the condition of following plans made by others that they refuse, inside and outside the factory. . . . It is not only neo-capitalist integration that is thrown into crisis.*"[7] Once you understand this crisis and break from the trade unionists, as well as the beginnings of a crisis and rupture within *Quaderni rossi* itself, which led to the split from Panzieri's group, you will see the first traces of the discourse of workers' autonomy.

Now we interrupt our chronology, going forward in time to Piazza Statuto, to then return to the crisis of *Quaderni rossi*. On July 7, 1962, a group of workers went to Piazza Statuto to attack the headquarters of the Unione Italiana del Lavoro (the Italian Union of Work), which had just signed yet another lousy contract with FIAT. Three days of battles with the police followed. Eleven years later, Potere Operaio would write that Piazza Statuto was their founding congress. The PCI and CGIL immediately denounced the protagonists as provocateurs, saying that they had been driven there in the bosses' luxury cars in order to instigate the fighting. This was nothing new: many struggles had before been denounced as led by outsiders, and many more would be again. And this paranoia about provocateurs shouldn't surprise us: the Left had denied the possibility of workers' autonomy to such an extent that, in a kind of Pavlovian reflex, every time the working class did its own thing it was immediately denounced as the work of undercover agents. What is interesting is rather the reasons that led the institutions of the workers' movement to denounce these particular struggles. They had for a long time maintained that the working class was irremediably defeated and that the factory was no longer a place of conflict. The gist was: they can't be workers because they don't behave like workers, they don't dress like workers, they are too young, and their hair is too long to be workers. In a certain sense the PCI and CGIL were telling the truth, the truth about themselves, a tragic truth: they hadn't understood anything about the new class composition that was emerging—its new figures, new behaviors, new needs and desires, and new forms of expression and conflict. They didn't even understand anything after these struggles had happened. They began to pose the problem of that specific class composition only when it was already in decline: when the mass worker shifted from a position of attack to one of defense in the 1970s, they used its icon against an even newer composition, whom they would dismiss as the "non-guaranteed."[8] This new composition of the social worker and future precarious workers, born out of the refusal of labor and out of struggles against the factory, would write the history of the 1970s.

Piazza Statuto split the editors of *Quaderni rossi*, who were accused of inspiring the clashes. The journal wrote an ambiguous communiqué, in which it distanced itself from the riots. We will now look more deeply into this double rupture (with the institutions of the workers' movement, on the one hand, and within *Quaderni rossi*, on the other), through the last two themes of this chapter: the concepts of *class composition* and *coresearch*.

The concept of class composition can be understood with regard to the Marxian category of the organic composition of capital, or rather in the relation between variable capital and constant capital. But, at the same time, it marks a point of radical discontinuity with this category, which is still stuck in Marx's vicious circle, namely, the risk of implying a deterministic symmetry between the structure of capital and the structure of the class. Rupture is central to class composition, or at least the possibility of rupturing that symmetry.

Class composition is the relationship between the capitalist articulation of the labor force, in its combination with machines, and the formation of the class as a collective subject. It is therefore the relationship between technical composition and political composition. But neither of these terms should be seen as static. Technical composition isn't a simple replica of the structure of exploitation, and political composition doesn't indicate an already realized autonomous subject. The articulation and hierarchization of the labor force are driven by workers' behavior, while the political formation of the class is in permanent tension between autonomy and subsumption. The social relation of capital, as an antagonistic relation, is as much within the technical composition as the political composition—it determines them and transforms them.

Neither are technical and political composition intended as a reworking of the relationship between class *in itself* and class *for itself*, which is mediated by consciousness. Both of these terms contain a supposed objectivity and teleology: in a classically dialectical relationship you pass from one to the other thanks to the actions of the party, which reveals to the workers what they already had even if they didn't know it. From Marx onward, class consciousness became the location of workers' truth, mystified and hidden by capitalism; a consciousness to be revealed more than created, belonging to the objectivity of History and not to the subjectivity of struggles. The mediation between the class *in itself* and the class *for itself* was therefore a function belonging exclusively to the party.

What is decisive in class composition is not consciousness, as an abstract attribute of class, but subjectivity. This is a question not of simply changing our vocabulary but of radically changing our perspective. Subjectivity goes beyond the simple facts of your origin, of your location within the labor process, or of your income, even if they clearly contribute to it. And it has nothing to do with psychology and psychoanalysis, which would become popular in the following decades. It is, as Alquati says, "the system of beliefs, of visions and conceptions, of representations, of knowledge, of culture and meanings; of desires, of the imaginary and also of the passions and of the will, of options etc. A system characterized by historicity and sociality and therefore one that evolves as part of a process. *Formazione*[9] *also contributes toward producing and transforming subjectivity.*"[10] Far from being determined objectively, subjectivity is a battlefield between capitalist *formazione* (either structured or unstructured) and possible counter-*formazione*. It is therefore a central element of, and what is at stake in, a relationship of production, which is a relationship of force. Subjectivity (as we will also see in the last chapter, when we will talk about the limits of so-called post-operaismo) is not in itself antagonistic, in the same way that political composition isn't about affirming the immediate autonomy of the class. The point is to transform subjectivity into counter-subjectivity, and composition into recomposition (another crucial term that we will return to below). The category of class composition is not only central but foundational to operaismo. In his book *Storming Heaven*, Steve Wright correctly understands it as fundamental to the history of operaismo.[11]

Finally, coresearch. A very suggestive term, it is usually interpreted either as a particular type of workers' inquiry, as a radical use of sociology (coresearchers were disdainfully labeled "anarcho-sociologists" by the academic Left), or as intellectuals "going to the people."[12] Let's first look at what Alquati said at the time, in the already cited texts included in the first issue of *Quaderni rossi*. Coresearch is "a method of political action from below," the "transformation of objective forces into subjective forces," "an entrance into workers' conflicts in order to develop with these workers, within their—already ongoing or possible—actions (based on demands), their possible political development, gradually putting forward new demands as part of that action."[13] And: "There is an attempt to overturn the situation of a negative relationship between workers and the 'conscious vanguard' through the transformation of all of the very well-motivated and positive aspects of the refusal of external delegates. Thus, the aim is to form, through long-term work, political groups within the factory, which function because the workers themselves, united as producers, take up the reins of their political struggle to realize a system that supersedes the current one, toward a socialism to be built."[14] In these few lines you can already see how the mediation between the political project of coresearch, the Panzierian group, and the simple trade union perspective was destined to fail.

This is not the position of the spontaneists,[15] some of whom paradoxically began believing in solely external and parliamentary actions, and later thought that among the young forces in the factories there was a political consciousness that had already been given in the Marxist sense—"that pure consciousness that no one has today, and less than ever those left-wing intellectuals (who had denounced spontaneism) who project onto the concretely mythicized working class a series of historical categories in which they collect all the ideological repression of the isolation forced upon them by the system or by the guilt that they feel at a certain point for their capitulation to the bosses of the culture industry."[16]

Here we can see the outline of two decisive themes to which we will return in the next chapter. The first is the relationship between spontaneity and organization: that which appears spontaneous is actually organized, while that which is understood as organized can fall prey to the myth of spontaneism (starting with the concept of class consciousness). The second is the relationship between intellectuals and militancy in Alquati's radical critique of the intellectualism of the Left. We will build upon these themes in the following pages, aware of the fact that if we changed a few words, the lines just cited could be written today.

Here, in the context of the workers' spontaneous response to neo-capitalism, "coresearch reproposes itself not as a cultural fact, the 'anthropological' conscience of the areas and forms of life that use the Marxian method, but as a political fact spontaneously affirmed by the same subjects involved in the organizational effort of the groups of young FIAT workers and employees with whom we've had contact. Coresearch comes from structural dialectic as a response to the political-organizational problems that technological progress poses to the working class and to the revolutionary socialist political militant."[17] Coresearch's radical difference from sociology lies in its aim and process. We can counter-use the tools of the social sciences, breaking them and recomposing them in a new science of rupture, a workers' science, a partisan science. Unlike in its populist version, there is no belief in horizontality between militants and workers. In a system that continuously produces inequality, equality is always what is being fought for and not the point of departure. The difference and ultimate rupture within *Quaderni rossi* was based on the difference and ultimate rupture between workers' inquiry, even in its innovative Panzierian form, and coresearch. Panzieri's workers' inquiry called into question the aim but not the process of sociology, leaving it intact while trying to direct it toward other goals. He maintained sociology's separation between the production of knowledge and organization, in fact implying that the former must be represented by the latter (whether through a union or a party). In coresearch, on the contrary, the production of knowledge and organization are part of the same process, even if they are two distinct dynamics. The production of knowledge is therefore simultaneously the production of organization and of counter-subjectivity. Coresearch is this process of political revolutionary production.

It is precisely through this practice of coresearch that Alquati and his group, made up of Pierluigi Gasparotto, Emilio Soave, and Romolo Gobbi, were able to radically overturn the dominant point of view, seeing in that specific class composition a possibility that no one else had, anticipating a new terrain on which a battle would be fought not long afterward.

Panzieri talks of an "inchiesta a caldo" (an inquiry in the heat of the moment), which is an inquiry into a struggle that is already happening. But then there is always the risk that the militant arrives too late, that is, at the same time as the sociologist. Alquati, on the other hand, talks of a sort of "inchiesta tepida" (a tepid inquiry), in that gray zone in which struggles haven't yet happened but could, an inquiry that moves, therefore, with the time of anticipation, taking risks, playing with the possibility of combining the production of knowledge, the production of organization, and the production of counter-subjectivity.[18]

Forty years after the revolt of Piazza Statuto, Alquati was asked whether they, the operaisti, had expected it. Alquati responded, "We didn't expect it, but we organized it."[19] There is no better way to describe the aim of coresearch, or the style of the militant.

3 The Trajectory of *Classe operaia*

Operaismo in the strict sense began with *Classe operaia*. Steve Wright is correct to describe *Quaderni rossi* as its incubation period. Panzieri pushed the relation between class autonomy and the workers' movement institutions to a state of extreme tension, but then stopped there, with the hope—later revealed to be illusory—that the latter could be changed and put at the service of the former. As we saw in the previous chapter, Panzieri believed that rethinking political action meant beginning from the gap that had been created between the workers' movement institutions (the party and the trade unions) and the real movement of the class. But whereas Panzieri and his group thought that this gap should be overcome, others thought it should be widened.

The conflict within *Quaderni rossi*'s editorial committee was political, theoretical, practical, and even existential. From the beginning, there was a particularly acute tension between the Panzierians and the group of coresearchers, Alquati, Gasparotto, Gobbi, and Soave.

The former accused the latter of "extremism," going so far as to call them Zengakuren (a Japanese communist student organization, particularly active in the anticolonial struggle starting from the end of the 1940s, which laid the ground for Japan's 1968). The coresearchers reclaimed the name, provocatively turning it against Panzieri's group.[1]

What was at stake was the relationship with the workers' movement institutions. Panzieri claimed that Alquati and his comrades had a "biological hatred" of the Left, its parties, unions, and culture. The question of culture was particularly important, both in this period and throughout operaismo. Alquati discussed this in two interviews published in *Futuro anteriore*, in which he argues that "explicit culture"—based on specializing in the arts and humanities, such as philosophy, history, or literature—maintained a paradoxical hegemony within operaismo.[2] This is the result of, or at least a powerful residue of, the idealism of that lineage going from De Sanctis to Gramsci via Croce, which enveloped and shaped the entire course of Italian Marxism, and which Tronti had already radically called into question at the end of the 1950s. It is this tradition that gave rise to the paradoxical and contradictory character of explicit culture within operaismo, which would widen and deepen in the following decades.

Alquati argued that it was this position that led to the virulent Panzierian attack on the coresearchers as "brutes," "louts," and "barbarians." They were accused of not possessing the explicit culture distinctive to the Left and the Italian Marxist tradition or, worse still—as Alquati pointed out—of possessing it and refusing to show it. This perspective also helps us to better appreciate Alquati's radical critique of the role of the intellectual. We are referring to his critique not only of organic and left intellectuals but of a role that was now "becoming labor" within the mechanisms of the culture industry.[3] As we saw in the previous chapter, when faced with "becoming labor," and the servility that typically characterizes it, the intellectuals react with "all the ideological repression of the isolation forced upon them by the system or by the guilt that they feel at a certain point for their capitulation to the bosses of the culture industry."[4] They ideologically exhibit that aura of exclusivity that they were losing materially, which in left circles manifested itself as explicit culture. (In the next chapter we will see that intellectual proletarianization driven by class autonomy would become a central battlefield in the years that followed.) The limits and fractures of the micro-conflict within the editorial committee of *Quaderni rossi* preempted a much wider problem: the contradiction between the intellectual and the militant, which was present in operaismo and is still unresolved today. We will briefly explain this and then return to it later.

For many of the people we are discussing here, becoming a militant meant breaking with being an intellectual, or at least with being simply an intellectual. In this way culture lost the aura mentioned above; it was—as Asor Rosa said—"defleshed," reduced to the skeleton of its bourgeois structures and functions. It now could be used or, better, counter-used in the service of struggles and in proposals for the construction of a new science, a "workers' science," as the coresearchers did with the social sciences. It is in this vein that Umberto Coldagelli and Gaspare De Caro wrote the text "Alcune ipotesi di ricerca marxista sulla storia contemporanea" (Some hypotheses of Marxist research on contemporary history). Published in the third issue of *Quaderni rossi*, it was an attempt to apply this general line of research and method to a specific discipline, thereby calling the latter into question and moving the battle onto the terrain of enemy knowledge.

Most importantly, there was a refusal of the presumed universal character of science and culture, as Asor Rosa emphasized in his 1965 essay, "Elogio della negazione" (In praise of negation): "The 'workers' point of view' is the radical negation of the principle that a general science exists, just as a general interest doesn't exist in society distinct from capitalist interest."[5] Thus science is bourgeois science, culture is bourgeois culture, society is bourgeois society. The critique of bourgeois ideology can't mean replacing it with another ideology, as Tronti explains in his 1962 essay, "Marx Yesterday and Today," later included in *Workers and*

Capital. On the contrary, Marxism's fundamental error was considering itself as the ideology of the workers' movement. Ideology is always bourgeois. The starting point for the critique of ideology must be the destruction of every ideology: "Marx is not the *ideology* of the workers' movement but its *revolutionary theory*."[6] Lenin wrote that there can't be revolutionary movement without revolutionary theory. Tronti completes this by saying that there can't be revolutionary theory without revolutionary practice. The former is always a function of the latter; without practice, theory is nothing.

In Tronti, "the negative destruction of all *ideological* and *political* mystifications"[7] is expressed through legitimate violence. Let's look, for example, at some of the passages in the introduction to *Workers and Capital*, with the Brechtian title "La linea di condotta" (literally translated as "The course of action," which is the Italian title of Brecht's play, *The Decision*): "From the viewpoint of capital's interest, it is ideology that lays the basis for science; for this reason, it founds it as a generalising social science";[8] "In short, big industry and its science . . . are the battlefield itself. And so long as the enemy occupies that field, we must spray it with bullets, without crying over the roses that get destroyed along the way";[9] "We ought to attend this same school each day [that of Leninian initiative]; it is there that we will grow, it is there that we will prepare ourselves, until we manage to read things directly without the foul mediation of books, until we are able to violently reshape reality without the cowardice of the ponderous intellectual";[10] a book today may "contain an element of truth only on condition that it is written in full awareness that we are doing something rather dreadful."[11] Further on in *Workers and Capital* we find the famous passage on the sociologist, who "starts reading *Capital* from the end of Volume 3 and stops reading when the chapter on classes breaks off. Then, every now and then someone, from Renner to Dahrendorf, has a grand old time of completing what had remained incomplete, and what results from all this is libel against Marx, which should, at a minimum, be punished with physical violence."[12]

For operaismo, knowledge is an instrument, a tool to be turned into a weapon. Its usefulness depends not on ideological, aesthetic, or universalist criteria but on its functionality for struggle. All knowledge that helps the struggle is good, and all knowledge that doesn't help it is bad. As Tronti said: "Knowledge is connected to the struggle. Whoever has true hatred has truly understood."[13] Even earlier, in his introduction to Marx's *Scritti inediti di economia politica* (Unpublished writings on political economy), which came out in 1963, Tronti wrote:

> For the Marxist, the object of analysis is capitalism. But the *concept* of capitalism is at the same time the concrete *historical reality* of capitalist society. The object of study is also the reality to be fought against. In this positive contradiction we find the *happy tragedy* of the Marxist theorist, who finds themselves

> wanting to destroy the object of their own study; in fact, to study it in order to destroy it: the object of their analysis is their enemy. And this is the specific historical character of Marxist theory: *its tendentious objectivity*. This is, then, nothing other than the material situation of the worker, who finds themselves having to fight against that which they themselves produce, wanting to eliminate the conditions of their labor and break the social relations of their production.[14]

Intellectuals against themselves, struggling against their own object of study and therefore against their own condition. They must hate it in order to study it, they must study it in order to ultimately destroy it. In this process the intellectual stops being an intellectual and meets the materiality of the working class: "It is in this way that the Marxist theorist must tend to increasingly identify themselves with the historical existence of the collective worker: up to the point of feeling themselves to be an organic part, a necessary moment of the struggle of the working class; to the point of conceiving their own theoretical destruction as already a practical destruction, and their own thought as a material articulation of the revolutionary process."[15] Workers' science becomes the science of negation, of destruction, of refusal. It is in this destruction of being an intellectual that the operaist militant is produced.

Again, we see the rupture with the Left and its iconographic cult of knowledge, its reverence for culture and for the figure of the intellectual that represents it. It is ridiculous to claim that knowledge and culture are not commodities. They are very much so, are always more so, and always more fundamentally so. But like all commodities they have a twofold character and their own peculiarities: they are functional to capitalist accumulation but can be overturned and counter-used against it. Not simply used as they are, but "defleshed," transformed and turned against their roots, and so destroyed. Driven by hate, the operaist militants looked for knowledge that was useful for struggle wherever they could find it: in the enemy camp ("the weapons of proletarian revolt have always been taken from the bosses' arsenals")[16] or even among reactionaries who shared the revolutionaries' hatred of bourgeois society (as we've already seen, better a great reactionary than a small revolutionary). Hence the reactionaries and conservatives (real or considered to be such) that the operaisti used, from Musil to Mahler, from Jünger to Schmitt, and from Nietzsche to Gehlen, to name but a few.

On the other hand, this rupture with the role of the intellectual, with its condition and aims, was never completed. And so, with time, and over the course of many struggles, it closed up again. We will see this more clearly in the last chapter: the accumulation of militant knowledge, produced and acquired as a break with the intellectual condition, later became a means of constructing the role of the intellectual in a break with the militant condition. This question is posed *ex post* by

Asor Rosa, in a brief autobiographical note, in his historical preface to his already cited texts from the 1960s: "For someone like me who was then preparing to embark on the professional path of a critic and historian of Italian literature, and for this reason, while applying to teach at school and at university, committed themselves toward knowing as much as possible of that history (it would be more accurate to say, all of it—that was the way it was then), another problem was raised: what specific place should be given to that history, and to which people in particular who were part of it, that in some way corresponded to this general vision of historical conflict?"[17] Then, as an aside, the author confesses his amazement, even discomfort at the way in which "Marx and Engels were used to plundering the great literary figures of the past to support their theories and discoveries" in a "largely instrumental, parasitic, purely citational use of literature."[18] It is in fact we who should feel amazement and discomfort, at a militant operaist who previously called for the destruction of ideology and the uncovering of the bourgeois nature of culture, but who now criticizes those who, like Marx, did just that, plundering culture and using it instrumentally, turning the weapons from the bosses' arsenal against them. It isn't a good sign when someone cries over "the roses that get destroyed along the way."

Analyzing the biographical trajectories of these subjects is helpful: we have seen how a rupture in individual histories previously created the conditions for the possibility of the interweaving and creation of a collective history. But here we see that the break in a collective history created the conditions for individual histories to reemerge. On this subject Alquati says:

> What counts in these wretched little stories is that, despite certain Nietzschean positions against values and what is then reduced to value, for example, this son of a railway worker (Asor Rosa) apparently needed personal emancipation through a traditionally specialist entrance into academic humanist culture; hence in all of his "professional" practices he contradicted some of his transgressive boutades: he wanted to climb up to where I was born, whereas after my downfall and expulsion from that world I had contempt for it. Another issue was the importance that is given to one's profession: some of us put our professions in second or third place and others didn't have them at all: they had renounced them! And the question is also what profession one chooses: to survive, as quasi-proletarians, those of us who came from participatory research and coresearch tried to do work that could also help us in our political militancy![19]

This is a very important point, to which we will return.

Another fundamental variable in the history of operaismo is generational, in relation both to the militants and to the social figures on whom they gambled: the workers, those specific workers. On the militants' side, those who first set up *Quaderni rossi* and then *Classe operaia* were in their twenties at the beginning of the 1960s (with very few exceptions). They came from different family backgrounds: some were marked by a process of "declassing" (whom Alquati referred to as the "humiliated and insulted"); others wanted to escape their proletarian condition; and others wanted to break with their bourgeois or petit bourgeois origins. The generational element was a powerful lever for opening up a fresh perspective, different from the ideological incrustations and defeatist mindset of the previous generations.

In the previous chapter we saw how the young age of the workers at Piazza Statuto upset the icon that the PCI and trade unions had created of the worker ideal type. That's because the politicized and unionized workers to whom they referred, which for convenience we will call the *craft workers*, who had entered the factory as teenagers and developed their ideological "consciousness" there, were not young, or at least, if they were, their age was simply an anagraphic condition that had little effect on their behavior. With the "new forces" entering the factories, generational differences weren't simply anagraphic, but began to be political: they brought with them new behaviors, expectations, and forms of life. It was they, in their striped T-shirts, who kicked off at Piazza Statuto and fought in the streets of Genoa. It was they who would later characterize the long Italian '68. It was they, Alquati noted, who were also stirring up the base of the parties and the unions.

This generation had an "intrinsic *politicità*,"[20] to use an expression that Alquati would later develop. They had a material, subjective potential that didn't express itself in an already fully developed, explicit form, but which could create a new principle of political action.

The mass worker was young in this not exclusively sociological sense. It was young as a type of laborer, because it was in those years that it first filled the production lines of the big factories in Northern Italy in their turbulent passage to Taylorism-Fordism. It was young in the sense that it expressed a fresh subjectivity within the factory and society, which differed from the habitual codes and norms of behavior. In the factory-city of Turin it was not only young but also predominantly made up of immigrants from Southern Italy. Satisfying the public's desire for victimhood, left-wing literature and cinema would depict these immigrants with tear-jerking images, laden down with cardboard boxes of belongings, standing in front of signs saying "We don't rent to Southerners!" In the beginning they were also heavily ostracized by the local workers, above all by those considered to be the most "conscious," that is, by those who were members of the party and the trade unions. They saw them as extraneous and even hostile to the culture of the workers' movement and criticized them for their opportunism, because they often voted for the reactionary trade unions. They labeled them passive, because they rarely took part in strikes. They called them "Napuli" (meaning "Naples"), which in Turin at the time was used for all Southerners, regardless of where they were actually from. Clashes between the old and the new workers were common. Both the leaders and the base of the workers' movement depicted the new workers as a sort of reworking of Marx's description of the Parisian lumpenproletariat, a figure that was objectively prey to reactionaries.

An aside, which should already be clear but is worth repeating in order to avoid misunderstanding: the passage from the *craft worker* to the mass worker shouldn't be interpreted in linear and homogeneous terms. First, it took on different characteristics and temporalities in different places: to put it simply, the mass workers in Turin, Milan, and Porto Marghera were not the same. Second, we are not claiming that from a certain point in time the traditional figure of the worker became a simple obstacle to the advancement of struggles: the overlaps, hybridization, and alliances within the factories were much more complicated and contradictory than the term "passage" implies. Finally, as should already be clear, we are speaking of a qualitative and not a quantitative process: the centrality of the mass worker didn't depend on its numerical presence within the factories, nor on its being a majority of the labor force, which it would never be. It depended instead on the combination of its location in the nerve centers of capitalist accumulation and its subjective behaviors, with their potential for rupture and generalization.

Through the practice of coresearch the operaisti dug below the surface of apparent victimhood, foreignness, opportunism, and passivity. And even before the struggles at Piazza Statuto, they found that within the metaphorical cardboard boxes of the Southern migrants lay the material potential for struggle. It wasn't simply their conditions of poverty or economic necessity that had led them to move, but also, and, in some cases principally, their need and desire for change. Often they came from places with a better quality of life than that which they found in Turin, but they were driven to move in search of another world, which they ambiguously identified with the factory-city. They thus were not predestined to be victims, as the Left liked to think, and still thinks, but were instead a growing force.

They were clearly foreign to the culture of the workers' movement, although often bringing with them experiences and stories of other kinds of struggle, such as land occupations; the mobility of labor thus became the mobility of struggle. The migrants were considered by the operaisti not as migrants but as carriers of conflict, a plague bacillus. Their outsider status was not a limit but a possibility. Of course, it is true that this status often led them to vote for reactionary trade unions without reservations or guilt. But, at the same time, it indicated, even if in a confused way and without an explicit political form, the negation of traditional representation and thus the possibility of autonomous political initiative. Their opportunism really existed, but it was deeply ambivalent, because it was also the expression of a unilateral, concrete, direct, and immediate interest. And it is true that they didn't participate in the strikes. When the coresearchers asked them why, they said that striking didn't get you anywhere. In some situations, passivity becomes a form of struggle: it becomes refusal.[21]

This was the point, this was the gamble: turn victimhood into force, outsider status into unrepresentability, opportunism into taking sides, passivity into refusal. The cycle of struggles of the mass worker set this overturning in motion.

The operaisti weren't searching for the icon of a worker from the social communist tradition, a conscious, generous bearer of the universal general interest, who loved their work and was proud of their condition. On the contrary, they were looking for those "unconscious" workers who expressed a partisan interest, refused work, instinctively hated their condition, and therefore ended up hating the capital that produced it. As Tronti writes in his article "Factory and Society," in the second issue of *Quaderni rossi*: "The working class should materially discover itself to be a *part* of capital if it wants to then counterpose the *whole* of capital to itself. It must recognise itself as a *particular element* of capital if it wants to then present itself as its *general* antagonist. The collective worker stands counterposed not only to the machine, as constant capital, but to labor-power itself, as variable capital. It has to reach the point of having as its enemy the whole of capital, including itself as a part of capital."[22] Workers against themselves, who negated themselves as labor power, because their labor power belonged to the enemy—this was the force that the operaisti were looking for. The sacred icons of labor and the workers' movement had finally been shattered.

This meant the destruction of the universal function attributed to an abstract working class, its sacrifice for the general interest, for History, and for the socialist future. For universalism is actually the totality's own image of itself: it is pure ideology. There was no longer space for discourses about humanity, which were revealed as a mystification of particular bourgeois interests. Operaismo was therefore an irreducibly partial point of view, because the totality could only be understood, grasped, and fought by taking sides. As Tronti said: "They have already told us that there is nothing universally human in all that we propose. And they are right. Indeed, here there is nothing of the bourgeoisie's particular interest. Have you ever seen a working-class struggle with a platform of generically human demands? There is nothing more limited and partial, nothing less universal in the bourgeois sense, than the struggle which workers wage on the factory floor against their direct boss."[23] Workers' thought had to adopt a correct political posture in relation to society, "simultaneously both within and against society, a partial view that theoretically grasps the totality precisely as a struggle to destroy this totality in practice, a vital moment in all that exists and thus an absolute power of decision over its survival. And this, indeed, is the condition of workers as a class, faced with capital as a social relation."[24]

We should now locate this extraordinary discourse and capacity for anticipation within political intervention in workers' struggles. We considered the break within *Quaderni rossi* that followed Piazza Statuto. It was already clear at that point that the tension between the two factions of the journal couldn't last: the Panzierian group was frightened by an approach that was going to destroy all relations with the workers' movement institutions; the others—beginning with the Romans and the coresearchers—claimed that the time was ripe for direct intervention in the intensifying workers' struggles whose possibilities and subjective characteristics they had foreseen. In September 1962, after the Piazza Statuto riot, "'Cronache' e 'Appunti' dei Quaderni rossi" ("Chronicles" and "Notes" of *Quaderni rossi*) came out, an attempt at mediation that bore little fruit. In June of the following year another collective issue was published, after which the rupture was finally confirmed. Three more issues of the journal would be published, the last in the second half of 1965, a year after Panzieri's untimely death.

A crucial step in the process that would lead to *Classe operaia* was the publication and distribution of the newspaper *Gatto selvaggio* (Wildcat), which was written by Alquati and Gobbi and called itself the "Newspaper of workers' struggles at FIAT and Lancia." Coresearch took form within the conflicts in these factories: the subtitle of the newspaper was *Nel sabotaggio continua la lotta e si organizza l'unità* (In sabotage, struggle continues and unity is organized), referring to a workers' practice that already existed there. Following its publication, Alquati and Gobbi left Turin overnight, fleeing possible arrest warrants. Alquati went first to Milan and then to Genoa, where he stayed with Gianfranco Faina's group. Gobbi found refuge in Venice, where Negri treated him like a legend.

The topics of *Gatto selvaggio*, expressed there as political agitation, were taken up by Alquati in his article "Struggle at FIAT" in the first issue of *Classe operaia*. They can be summed up in the apparent oxymoron "organized spontaneity." It wasn't external organization that produced conflict and it wasn't simple spontaneity that drove it. A sort of "invisible organization" had been created through which the workers communicated, prepared struggles, scheduled their attacks, and blocked the factory. It was this invisible organization that was the avant-garde in the processes of recomposition, while the party militants followed hesitantly and in fact often acted as an obstacle: "The wildcat strike at FIAT liquidates the old idea that, at this level, the workers' struggle would be organized by a particular internal 'nucleus' that holds a monopoly on antagonistic workers' consciousness. The strike of October 15–16 [1963] was organized directly by the entire and compact 'social mass' of workers from the sections that contributed: but we are here merely presented with greater clarity a characteristic of recent struggles, one that's not exclusive to FIAT where the rare 'militants' of the old parties after the June of '62 were just the tail-end of the struggles."[25]

The wildcat struggles that fed off invisible organization were unpredictable, and so couldn't be controlled by reformist mediation. They were realized through a continual rotation of tactics, methods, times, and places, and "demand[ed] nothing."[26] Although they were the most advanced level of worker "non-collaboration," they were not of course the only form of struggle—there were also mass strikes and clashes in the streets. The problem was combining and reinvigorating these struggles, ensuring that they mutually reinforced one another: "The task of a political organization is not to plan the wildcat in a predetermined way, because that seriously runs the risk of domesticating it, thus rendering it recuperable for the boss: the organization must instead contribute to intensifying it, while in order to organize and extend it, it's enough to have the 'invisible organization' of workers for whom the wildcat strike is becoming a permanent fact."[27]

In the traditional Marxist dialectic between spontaneity and organization, the former, in a linear succession of stages of development, gives way to the necessary intervention of the latter. Thanks to their experience of struggles within and against Taylorism-Fordism, the coresearchers showed that this linear succession meant that struggles lost their strength, opening the way to a mediation deprived of any force for rupture. Bosses are given control over timing, and the struggles become predictable and easily coopted. Contrary to what those who support the fetish of the party like to think, there is in fact no split that has to be dialectically recomposed between immediate interests and the final aim of struggle. However, neither is there an immediate identity between the two, as held by those faithful to the cult of spontaneity. There is instead a remainder that is wholly internal to the processes of struggle and organization. It is within this remainder that the militant coresearcher acts and plans. As Alquati put it, the unity of working-class movements is fully implied in the new forms of struggle. The only way to verify this is to begin to organize it. It is the political line that creates organization and not vice versa. After all, as Alquati claimed in his presentation to the PSI congress in 1961, "a political line is not an object, it is a guide that gives perspective to daily work. It is a process in which all of the problems of the next step are determined, which will take us to the new line corresponding to the new situations that the previous phase prepared. And that applies, for example, to organization, which in its turn is not a thing, an object, but a moment in the process of class struggle."[28]

Three years later, coresearch was that daily work and had become that process.

In January 1964 the first issue of *Classe operaia* came out, describing itself as the "political monthly of workers in struggle." Direct intervention in workers' struggles was partly a reality and partly a desire. It existed in Turin in the forms we've just mentioned and also at the petrochemical complex in Porto Marghera through a group of comrades who were particularly significant in *Classe operaia* and later in Potere Operaio. This latter group, which included Negri, Luciano Ferrari Bravo, and Guido Bianchini as well as militants working in the factory, would give rise to one of the most important concrete experiences of workers' autonomy in Italy in the '60s and '70s.[29] In addition to the Romans, the newspaper also included the Genoese group, who, as we have just seen, gathered around Gianfranco Faina; the Florentine group—Claudio Greppi, Lapo Berti, Luciano Arrighetti, and Giovanni Francovich; and the Milanese group—Sergio Bologna, Giairo Daghini (who was originally from Switzerland), and Mauro Gobbini (originally from Rome). All of these groups experimented with different forms of intervention in the factories. And we mustn't forget Mario Mariotti's exceptional cartoons, which illustrated the paper's arguments.

The first issue of *Classe operaia* opened with "Lenin in England," a now-famous editorial written by Mario

Tronti. Its most well-known passage describes the operaist overturning of our point of view, a definitive change of orientation with respect to the Marxist tradition: "We too saw capitalist development first and the workers second. This is a mistake. Now we have to turn the problem on its head, change orientation, and start again from first principles, which means focusing on the struggle of the working class. At the level of socially developed capital, capitalist development is subordinate to working-class struggles; not only does it come after them, but it must make the political mechanism of capitalist production respond to them."[30] At this stage in the book, we don't need to explain this overturning again, as we've already seen it at work in the anticipatory practices and ruptures of the operaisti. The Left's interest in victimhood was not only destroyed but also forcefully turned on its head: capital was the servant; the working class was the master. Only the workers could be autonomous: capital would always be subordinate to struggles. Only by responding to them could it find the form for its own development. But the servant dominates and forces the master to work for them, to think like them, to behave like them: capital imposes its slave morality on the workers.

On the basis of this foundation of a method, a point of view, Tronti criticizes developmentalism and antidevelopmentalism, both Marxist teleology and Third Worldist theology. It isn't true that you can always read in the human being its origins in the ape. If this were the case, then everything could be explained and resolved where capitalism is most advanced, in the United States. And neither is it true that the epicenter of the revolution should be looked for in the weakest link of capital, namely, among those who are most oppressed (Third Worldism, with its love of the weak and its humanitarian compassion, is as far as you can get from operaismo). Tronti's thesis was that the chain could now be broken not where capital was weakest but where the working class was strongest. Italy was at a dynamic middle point, in the midst of international capitalist development and with significant working-class power; it could therefore "become a moment for the subjective unification of different and opposed levels of struggle."[31] The Center Left government, which came into power just before *Classe operaia* was founded, could be read as a response to class struggle. It was a reformist response, which exposed the mystificatory character and inevitable destiny of reformism: it aimed for the planned management of capital, whereas capital actually develops only through leaps and ruptures.

Obviously, the factory and not parliament was where workers' power should be put into action. Or rather, as Tronti argued, the machine of the bourgeois state had to be broken within the capitalist factory. This was a starting point that could then lead to the possibility of a generalization of workers' struggles across the entire society, which was also increasingly becoming factory-like.

He had already foreseen this in his article "Factory and Society," which opened the second issue of *Quaderni rossi*. "At the highest level of capitalist development, this social relation becomes a *moment* of the relation of production, the whole of society becomes an *articulation* of production, the whole society lives in function of the factory and the factory extends its exclusive dominion over the whole society."[32]

However, there was still some distance between the "new laws of action," which would be laid out in *Workers and Capital* in 1966, and the reality of direct intervention in the cycle of struggles of the mass worker, which would remain rather limited and circumscribed. Differences in perspective soon emerged within the editorial committee of *Classe operaia*. Although its members seemed to agree that strategy belonged to the class and tactics to the party, the question remained as to which tactics and what party. For Negri the workers were "without allies," as can be seen in the editorial he wrote for the third issue of the newspaper. Alquati argued that, through struggle, the class becomes autonomous to the extent that it separates itself not only from the movements of capital but also from the objective articulation of the labor force. Thus, in recomposing itself the class becomes autonomous and tendentially able to detach itself from the technical composition. The question of organization should be posed by beginning from this autonomy. Although starting from the same assumption, Tronti saw things differently, a position that he summarized forty years later in an interview published in *Futuro anteriore*:

Actually with *Classe operaia* I had something else in mind, I think it should have been a very intense experience, very concentrated in time, that should have practically formed—precisely at the level of direct contact with workers' struggles, and so at the right level—a sort of managing group that would then, after that experience, reenter big politics. I had in mind the creation of a group of strong political personalities to quite openly reenter the Communist Party as a nucleus that, because of its force, its *formazione*, and its decisiveness would be able to tip the balance of the PCI toward becoming a more revolutionary party.[33]

As further issues were published, other differences clearly began to emerge, at least internally. In September 1964 there was talk of an "Italian 1905"—comparing the workers' struggles at the time to the political tremors of the first Russian revolution, with the tactical objective of gathering together the forces needed for a successive revolutionary phase—which reopened discussions about the Communist Party. The December 1964 issue was dedicated to the theme of "class and party," moving between discussions of the workers' use of the party and the requalification of the role of the party within and against the state. The gap between this position and the hypothesis of the autonomous organization of the class widened in the following two years. The final issue came out in March 1967, and, without revealing any major fractures, soberly announced the end of the newspaper, predicting that the 1960s in Italy would finish early since they had already had their time. "The rich content of struggles, of massified forms, the strong continuity of the movement, the open character of conflict and the significant results that were provisional but concrete: we need to start from there, not, as is often done, to theorize about the necessary ebb and flow of the movements of workers' struggles, but to prepare ourselves for and anticipate the next possible leap forward."[34] The editorial "classpartyclass" finished with an explicit "till we meet again": "Now we are going. There is a lot for us to do. In our heads, we carry a monumental project of research and study. And politically, finding our feet again on solid ground, we need to seize the new level of action. *It will not be easy.*"[35] This goodbye would take different and even opposing paths, which we will discuss in the next chapter.

4 Operaismo beyond Operaismo

Operaismo in the strict sense, which was nurtured in *Quaderni rossi* and fully developed in *Gatto selvaggio* and *Classe operaia*, came to an end in 1967. This is Tronti's thesis: *Quaderni rossi* and *Classe operaia*. Stop. Then another story begins.[1] Negri shared this analysis, although coming to very different conclusions, which he laid out in the introduction to the 1979 edition of *Classe operaia*.[2] Alquati also agreed that the collective experience had ended, but followed neither Tronti "within and against" the PCI nor the Venetians and others in their journey toward Potere Operaio.

Yet, only a few months after the publication of the final issue of *Classe operaia*, the Italian "long '68" began. It was in many ways unique at the international level, particularly with its mix of student revolts and workers' struggles in the years '68 and '69 (from Veneto, via Valdagno and Porto Marghera, to Corso Traiano in Turin). This cycle of struggle lasted longer in Italy than in other parts of the world and led to the formation of new conflictual subjects. It could be said to be bookended by the events of 1968 and 1977, although reducing everything to these symbolic dates risks simplifying much wider and longer-term processes.

As a result of the different political perspectives that led to the end of *Classe operaia*, there is quite a substantial divergence in analyses of the events of 1968 and the political phase that followed. Writing at the end of the 1990s, in *La politica al tramonto* (Politics at sunset), Tronti described their "happy blunder": "From the workers' struggles to protest movements, it was as if a red curtain fell and ended the theater of an epoch. To us, to many, it seemed instead that an epoch was opening.... There was a redness on the horizon: it's just it was not the glow of the dawn, but of the twilight." The blunder was a happy one because it meant the end of the representation of the old world. However, the curtain also closed on the "great 20th century": the political exhaustion of the workers' movement took with it the possibility of "great politics." Afterward, Tronti wrote, everything would be small: the small twentieth century, small politics. He concluded that theory and practice needed to be reassessed: slowing down on the curve of practice, speeding up on the straight road of theory.

For Potere Operaio, both in its first local group in Veneto and Emilia, as well as in its later national organization, that redness was the dawn. An autonomous dawn within the factory, as seen in Porto Marghera, and a possible dawn outside it, at the universities thrown into disarray by the students. Most of the operaisti believed that the students had to get behind the workers' struggles. If not, '68 would risk becoming a mere tool for the modernization of Italy, which Tronti argues it eventually became.

Based on their experience of May '68 in Paris, Sergio Bologna and Giairo Daghini published "Maggio '68 in Francia" (May '68 in France) in *Quaderni piacentini*, a long text that remains a key point of reference for understanding the political significance of 1968 on both sides of the Alps.[3] In those days of metropolitan insurrection, we can see the first traces of the consolidation of the student-worker relationship, pointing toward the movement's character of mass political unification and its rethinking of revolution.

In the same period, beginning from his research at Olivetti, Sergio Bologna started to develop his discourse on technicians, who in some ways bridged the figures of the worker and the student. Alquati had already explored this role in his inquiries within and against the factory in the town of Ivrea, in which he highlighted the growing contradiction between the socialization of the production process and the increasingly political function of capitalist hierarchy. For the October 1965 issue of *Classe operaia*, Bologna wrote "Il discorso sui tecnici" (Discourse on technicians), in which he challenged the idea—widespread within the trade unions—of the technician as the most politically advanced figure within the hierarchy of capitalist production.[4]

These reflections contained important arguments both for defeating the mythologies of the social communist tradition and for further defining the relationship between technical class composition and political class composition. They called into question the iconic image of the worker, which was reduced to their physicality, to nerves and muscles, as if the truth of class location was to be found in their dirty overalls. At the same time, they also criticized the idea that capitalist hierarchy determined the hierarchy of struggles, which implied a messianic wait for the necessary explosion of conflict at the most advanced points of capitalist production. This was the same position that, in the 1930s, had meant technicians—or whichever workers had the most advanced professional skills—were made the heads of the party cells in the Soviet factories. The reason technicians were a potentially political figure in that specific phase was because they were situated along a possible fault line of crisis within the capitalist division of labor. The growing socialization of productivity made their behavior increasingly similar to that of the other workers, and so their ambiguous interests could come into conflict with those of the bosses. But it is not class location that determines struggle; it is struggle that determines class location. As Tronti said, *there is no class without class struggle*.

Thus, there isn't any symmetrical or deterministic obverse relationship between technical composition and political composition. The central figure in the political composition isn't necessarily the central figure in the technical composition. Once again, we need to turn our point of view on its head, change orientation. As we saw, the centrality of the mass worker in a specific phase was given by its intrinsic refusal and potential antagonism in the hub of the productive process in which it was situated. If those behaviors were weakened, domesticated, or recuperated, then the mass worker would lose its political centrality.

Struggles also give the wage a political function. There are historical phases in which it doesn't have that function, or in which it is reduced to trade union negotiation, and so does not affect the general relations of force between the classes. But in other phases the wage ceases to be a mere contractual question, becoming instead both the battlefield on which struggles for power are fought and the spoils of war. This was the case in the struggles of the mass worker. In the slogan "Equal pay increases for all!," the stress is on the affirmation of equality, independent of the capitalist hierarchy and the technical composition. The same goes for "More money, less work!," in which there is an immediate demand for power: we don't want a "fair" wage, linked to work and productivity; we want money that is decoupled from work and productivity, a demand that is thus tendentially against labor and productivity. In the 1970s, with the political growth of what would come to be known as the "social worker," the battlefield shifted toward the appropriation of a "social" income,[5] or rather an immediate demand for power.

Let's return to the operaist groups, which at this point were suffering internal splits. Between May and August 1969, *La classe* was founded, a weekly "newspaper of worker and student struggles." Although only thirteen issues were published, its significance should not be underestimated. It was produced in Turin, where people from Porto Marghera, Milan, and Rome had temporarily moved. It was here that those who would go on to form Potere Operaio first came together in the organization of struggles, including Negri, Bologna, Daghini, Emilio Vesce, Franco Piperno, Oreste Scalzone, Ferruccio Gambino, Lauso Zagato, and Alberto Magnaghi. They were also joined by Mario Dalmaviva, who had recently moved from Rome to Turin, a militant with direct links to the struggles at FIAT and a member of the Student-Worker League. As he said in his interview in *Futuro anteriore*, he was educated through struggle: "[I was] not at all typical because I wasn't born into a communist or socialist or union family: it was a question of taking sides, which involved a bit of adventure, a bit of superficiality. Basically, I saw that the world was changing and I had no desire to stay put."[6] In other words: "O gentlemen, the time of life is short ... An if we live, we live to tread on kings."[7]

In the brief but intense experience of *La classe*, a division first arose between that which would become Potere Operaio and that which would become Lotta Continua (a name coined by Dalmaviva), becoming clearer in the "National Meeting of the Vanguard of Workers and Students," which took place in Turin toward the end of July 1969. On the third day of that month, a housing protest by workers and students going from the FIAT factory of Mirafiori to the dormitory suburb of Nichelino ended in hours of fighting with the police on Corso Traiano, in one of the most highly symbolic events of the Italian '68–'69.

In January 1968, the first issue of *Contropiano* was published, a quarterly founded by Asor Rosa, Negri, and Massimo Cacciari, with contributions from Tronti and di Leo, among others. There Negri laid out his already well-known critique of the relationship with the PCI and the workers' movement institutions in two important essays, which would later be republished in *Operai e stato*: "Keynes and the Capitalist Theory of the State Post-1929" and "Marx on Cycle and Crisis."[8] From a solidly operaist perspective, Negri explained how Keynesianism was a response not to capital's internal contradictions but to the enormous threat posed by the Bolshevik October. Unlike the other journals that we've discussed, *Contropiano* was not linked to political intervention, either hypothetical or real; its battles were on the cultural terrain, aimed at appropriating the "great thought" of crisis and bourgeois decadence, which were marked by strong irrational or openly conservative elements.

The newspaper *Potere operaio*, whose first issue came out in September 1969, had a completely different function: it was directly concerned with organization and linked to political intervention. Over the course of its publication there were three different versions: the weekly, the monthly, and *Potere operaio del lunedì* (Monday's *Potere operaio*). Potere Operaio was made up of various political groups in the northern and central regions of Italy, but, despite various attempts, it had problems taking off in the South. It nevertheless found a relatively wide following, while being marked by discontinuities with the operaist experiences that had preceded it. This was to be expected, as there was already discontinuity due to changes in class composition: the struggles of the mass worker, which seemed to be at their peak, were actually already in decline.

The story of Potere Operaio[9] is symbolically delimited by Corso Traiano at its outset and, in March 1973, the "red handkerchiefs" of Mirafiori,[10] which marked its end. The latter led to occupations, strikes, protests, and blockades: a struggle not for work but against work, with behaviors and a subjectivity that—although starting from within the factory—already signaled a shifting of *operaietà* onto the social plane.[11]

Potere Operaio placed a lot of importance on developing international links, so much so that it had an international commission. We will list just a few of these links: with Germany, most importantly through Sergio Bologna and his relationship with Karl Heinz-Roth, a militant and the author of *L'altro movimento operaio* published in *Materiali Marxisti*;[12] with the United States and Canada, particularly with the League of Revolutionary Black Workers in Detroit;[13] and with France and Switzerland, most notably with Yann Moulier-Boutang and Christian Marazzi.[14]

Potere Operaio also had an important relationship with the new wave of feminism nascent in Italy at the time. Alisa Del Re and Mariarosa Dalla Costa had been part of the organization, but in 1972, along with other women in the group, left to form Lotta Femminista. The group was involved in the international Wages for Housework campaign, or perhaps it would be better to say *against* housework, which in some ways was an operaist version of feminism, linked to struggles and demands made by "workers in the home."[15]

Now let's look at Potere Operaio's relationship with Lotta Continua, led by Adriano Sofri. As much as the group contained an operaist echo (Sofri had had close links with *Classe operaia* and *La classe*, and his group in Pisa was even called Potere Operaio), Lotta Continua clearly differed from Potere Operaio. In Lotta Continua people came together from different backgrounds, some with links to social Catholicism, with a discourse that was more populist—in the traditional sense of the term—than class-related. This led the group to make some significant interventions, for example, in Southern Italy, during the Reggio Calabria riots,[16] as well as through their call to "Take back the city!," which expressed an urgent need to go beyond the factory. Antifascism, a practice and ideology that characterized many groups at the time, was also a strand in Lotta Continua's chaotic organization. The myths of the Resistance, whether considered to have been betrayed or to be repeated in the face of new hypothetical authoritarian turns, pointed toward the option of armed struggle. For Potere Operaio, and later for Autonomia, there was no theoretical space for an antifascist discourse (although, in practice, antifascism was necessary in some regions due to the strength of fascist groups in those areas, it was generally considered to be a backward, democratic, Frontist, and national-popular position, in contrast with the centrality of the class relationship). On the other hand, antifascism was used by the PCI against the autonomous movements, whom they called the "*diciannovisti*," implying their similarity with those who set up the first fascist movement in 1919, which managed to hegemonize the widespread opposition to the status quo that followed the First World War.[17] The infamous image of the security section of the PCI defending the shrine of the partisans from the autonomists was later emblematic of 1977 in Bologna. The partisans had been disembodied, separated from their conflictual *politicità* and concrete subjectivity. They had been reduced to empty icons to be used against those who embodied a new conflictual subjectivity.

Between 1972 and 1973 the crisis within Potere Operaio grew, along with similar crises in other groups. There are multiple reasons for this, beginning from its organizational form. In most descriptions of that period there is a tendency to highlight the disagreements around the hypothesis of the insurrectional party, which after the break in the May 1973 conference in Rosolina led those linked to Negri to set up Autonomia, while others tried to keep Potere Operaio going. The latter included Piperno and the Romans, the Florentines, and, initially, the Venetians. There were also others, such as Bologna, Daghini, Berti, and Franco Berardi Bifo, who had already left, deeply critical of what they saw as an increasingly hyper-organizational rigidity.

Independently of the evaluations we might make of particular operaist groups, they shared a general limit: although on a theoretical and sometimes practical plane they were able to anticipate emerging movements, characteristics, and subjectivities in the changing class composition, they had difficulty translating this into an appropriate organizational form. In fact, we could say that organization was the black hole of all the operaist groups. And the same can be said of the different declinations of Autonomia: although there were important experiments in organizing the social worker at a local level, they never had more than a fragmentary character.[18]

On the other side, we have Tronti, "within and against" the party, who would propose the hypothesis of the autonomy of the political, beginning from the assumption that the class, even in the peak of its struggles, couldn't make it alone: a tool was needed to allow for action within and against the state, just as the workers' struggle acted within and against the factory and society. For Tronti this was implicit in the operaist experience, as he explained in his interview in *Futuro anteriore*: "That the operaist subjectivity should develop a political theory that was as strong as its social subjectivity, therefore a strong theory of politics that was a realistic theory of politics, this was something that was already implicit earlier and which the discourses on the autonomy of the political simply made explicit, and which is not in any way in conflict with the operaist experience. But that was quite a lonely road: while operaismo created and recreated a collective, this discourse on the autonomy of the political was quite a solitary experience. There was a group of young collaborators, but it wasn't at all comparable with the collective that wrote the operaist journals which we're talking about."[19] Tronti's analyses are important from a theoretical point of view, in his rereading of the thinkers of modern politics, from Machiavelli and Hobbes up to Carl Schmitt. But in their translation into practice, as Tronti says in the same passage, they didn't have tangible results. In the PCI, on the other hand, the autonomy of the political was transformed into the autonomy of the party against the autonomy of class, in a reactionary overturning of the original operaist hypothesis. Or, to simplify this in Schmittian terms, we could say that politics as administration immediately absorbed politics as conflict. The general problem was that politics didn't become a weapon with which to act within a process but was instead a separation from that process. Even if we do not share his conclusions, the question and the problem that Tronti's hypothesis posed have remained unanswered.

Let's return to the last days of Potere Operaio. The militants who broke away at the 1973 conference in Rosolina went on to form what would become Autonomia Operaia Organizzata, which grew out of a number of factory interventions, such as the autonomous assembly at Porto Marghera and the workers' collectives at Alfa Romeo, Face Standard, and Sit-Siemens in Milan. There they met the Gruppo Gramsci, which was also disbanding. The latter group had more classically Marxist-Leninist leanings, and included Romano Màdera, Giovanni Arrighi, Carlo Formenti, and Paolo Gambazzi. The document announcing their dissolution was significantly entitled: "Dal Gruppo all'Organizzazione dell'autonomia operaia: Fare un passo in avanti!" (From the Group to the Organization of Autonomia Operaia: Taking a Step Forward!). Not long before, the Gruppo

Gramsci had published the first issue of the newspaper *Rosso*. After the meeting between the two groups *Rosso* changed its orientation, now describing itself as the "newspaper within the movement." Again, we see the characteristic operaist position: the attempt to create a space of possibility within the crisis, seizing the opportunity for a leap forward. However, a few years later, the former leaders of the Gruppo Gramsci left, while the newspaper became the reference point for Autonomia Operaia Organizzata.

In the meantime, *Rosso* (almost exclusively active in the North) had become closer to the Comitati Autonomi Operai in Rome, which in 1974 started the newspaper *Rivolta di classe*. This alliance ended before 1977, and the following year the Comitati Autonomi Operai set up the paper *I Volsci*. It published eleven issues, ending in October 1981, and gave voice to struggles within the service sector and to those against illegal employment and nuclear energy. The Comitati had a genealogy that was different from that of the other groups we have mentioned: they came not from Potere Operaio or operaismo but from various political backgrounds (one of its leaders, Vincenzo Miliucci, was a militant in the *Il manifesto* group[20]). They had a position that could be called movementist or Luxemburgist. Their debates on organization were symptomatic of the aftermath of 1977: *I Volsci* published an article entitled "Per il Movimento dell'Autonomia Operaia" (For the Movement of Autonomia Operaia) complete with a suggestive acronym (MAO), while *Rosso* reaffirmed the hypothesis of the creation of a party (later the Collettivi Politici Veneti[21] would propose the formation of an "organized communist movement" in their newspaper *Autonomia*). Both positions came up against the limits of translation into practice. From its inception, *Rosso* paid attention to the new questions raised by the young proletariat and to the transformations taking place in production with the decline of the mass worker and the theorization of the new figure of the "social worker." It focused on the experiments not only in the cities, but also in the provinces, for it was there that the "diffused social factory" was developing. We should here mention the network of groups in the provinces of Varese and Como in Lombardy, and the experiences of the Collettivi Politici Veneti, which were the longest-lasting in terms of organization and local impact (and which, as we have seen, began from the continuation of Potere Operaio[22]—in fact, in November 1977, the subtitle of *Rosso* became "Per il potere operaio" [For workers' power]). The final issue came out in May 1979. In that same year, on April 7 and December 21, a number of comrades from the former Potere Operaio and from the Autonomia groups were arrested.

Those who had wanted to continue with Potere Operaio at Rosalina kept it going for a few years. In 1974, during the second occupation of FIAT, *Fuori dalle linee* (Outside the lines) came out. In July 1975, a single-issue journal, *Linea di condotta* (Course of action) was published, proposing the recomposition of the remaining fragments of Potere Operaio. Its subtitle was "materials on the crisis and workers' organization": once again we have crisis and organization, the overturning of the former creating a possibility for the latter. This was the aim, the unsolved problem.[23] Four years later, in June 1979 (in the wake of the events of April 7 in which a number of the editors of *Linea di condotta* were arrested, due to their being militants in Potere Operaio), the journal *Metropoli* was set up by some of the same people: this time there was an attempt to introduce the hypothesis of a "possible autonomia" to those who had taken part in the '77 movement, aiming at developing analyses of new forms of subjectivity and of the crisis of salaried labor. *Metropoli* also had a sister publication, *Preprint*, which focused on theoretical discussion. Between '75 and '78, Scalzone's group, which had also left Potere Operaio, set up *Senza tregua* (No truce), which was centered in Milan, in particular around the political intervention at the Magneti Marelli factory. The newspaper was related to the Comitati Comunisti per il potere operaio, with one of its central themes (associated with concrete practice) being the "autonomous control of the territory."

Various other groups emerged from operaismo that were more or less linked to concrete organizational trajectories. Of particular importance was *Primo Maggio*

(First of May), founded in 1973 by Bologna, Cartosio, and Franco Mogni. The journal placed itself outside the different positions and groups, with the aim of reflecting on and debating important new questions (for example, the discourse on Marx and money, in which Bologna's, Marazzi's, and Berti's contributions stand out, as well as some initial research on transport and logistics). It also aimed to create a militant historiography, which from the start had an international dimension (for example, the research on workers' struggles in the United States and the Industrial Workers of the World, for the most part carried out by Cartosio). The journal was still being published well after the 1970s, with the twenty-ninth and final issue coming out in autumn 1988. Another notable publication was *La tribù delle talpe* (The Tribe of Moles), edited by Bologna, which included a very rich and original analysis of the '77 movement.

And we mustn't forget *A/traverso*, which was founded in 1975 as a supplement to *Rosso*, largely at the initiative of Bifo and the Bolognese "creative autonomia" movement. With a distinctive graphic style, the focus was on the problems of language and on the new youth composition. It criticized ideologies and organizations, the oppressive role of the PCI, and really existing socialism, with a strong emphasis on the refusal of work. *A/traverso*, together with Radio Alice, played an important role in the '77 movement in Bologna.[24]

The above summary outlines the role played by newspapers and journals in the 1960s and 1970s, showing how, for the most part, they were instrumental both to the organization of discourse and for political practice.[25] Even more importantly, they were often direct expressions of organization.

This chapter closes with a key theme: the social worker. For Negri, it indicated the homogeneity between the concept of the salaried worker and the concept of the productive worker, or rather the social nature of productive labor, which results in the constitution of a unified proletariat.[26] Even if this category points to the basis of the process of recomposition in the unity of abstract social labor, the roles and behaviors that the social worker incarnated were far from abstract: the young proletariat, the intellectual proletariat, and workers breaking away from the factory and escaping the slavery of the wage relation. In short, it was the universe of the refusal of work. The PCI pejoratively called them the "non-guaranteed" and the "second society," in another tired re-proposition of the idea of the objectively reactionary character of the lumpenproletariat. Instead, it now saw itself as the representative of the mass worker, which it had failed to understand when it was conflictual, only embracing it as an icon now that it was defeated and sheltering in defensive positions. On February 17, 1977, the security section of the trade unions defended a rally held by Luciano Lama, the secretary of the CGIL, against the autonomists. The resulting clash symbolically expressed a conflict within the class composition.

Alquati was perhaps the first to analyze the category of the social worker, a year before the events of '77, in his lengthy essay "L'università e la formazione. L'incorporamento del sapere sociale nel lavoro vivo" (The university and *formazione*: The incorporation of social knowledge in living labor), which was published in issue 154 of *Aut aut*. This thesis would be further developed in the important book *Università di ceto medio e proletariato intellettuale* (Middle-class university and the intellectual proletariat), written by Alquati in collaboration with Nicola Negri and Andrea Sormano. The social worker was a subject born at the crossroads between struggles in the factory and social struggles; from the incorporation of social knowledge in living labor and from the ambivalent practices of self-valorization; between autonomy and individualization, between reappropriation and professionalization. It was precisely the autonomous appropriation of social knowledge that forced capital to take a leap forward in the industrialization of knowledge production, posing "this autonomous valorization as the privileged parameter within which the bosses must adaptively construct new forms for the general organization of the productive processes, and in their restructuring of command through technology."[27] The intellectual proletariat, for Alquati, were the various hundreds of thousands of young proletarians of working age (often as young as twenty years old) who increasingly fill the middle and high schools and the university. Why are they proletarians? Because they can only live by commodifying and reselling their labor power, which others use and consume for their own exclusive advantage without even worrying about the production and reproduction of this precious and badly paid commodity. They are proletarians both due to their present condition and due to their background. They are proletarians who have a high level of schooling and rightly do not like the conditions of today's worker, which they almost always have already experienced.[28]

Alquati argues that it is wrong to identify the social worker with a part or a fragment, with the tertiary worker or the service worker, because the utility of this category is in its "defining the *new general form* of the working class in its present recomposition."[29] Defining, that is, the possible tendency that characterizes them in the sense of *operaietà*, which has never had anything to do with calloused hands and dirty overalls, but with the identification, within the proletarian class, of a potential conflictual and recompositional force. Again, as with the mass worker, the social worker's possible centrality was given not by quantity but by quality, or rather not by its role within the capitalist articulation of the labor force but by its capacity to attack, which can be expressed in its struggles against being reduced to labor power: "The mass worker, and even before that the craft worker, taught us that hegemony is not in the quantity, but in the quality of the relationship within accumulation and within the struggle against accumulation."[30] Its centrality, then, depends on the subjective potential of its role of rupture and recomposition within specific hubs of capitalist valorization.

This figure finds a point of solidity and possible application of its power in the new university, which Alquati defines as containing a middle class in a crisis of mediation—a middle class that under the force of autonomia operaia had been broken up and polarized, no longer capable of carrying out its traditional function as a dam for containing class struggle. For this reason, Alquati argues that the university played a key role, as a hinge between factory, society, and state, within a process of capitalist restructuring and rationalization that wasn't limited to the production and management of surplus value, but which had as its principle objective the disarticulation of the previous class recomposition. It was thus the place to be attacked. Anticipating this process, already in 1968—unlike the operaisti who insisted on the exclusive centrality of workers' struggles in the factory, running the risk of transforming a tactical question into a strategic orthodoxy—Alquati criticized the procession of students toward the factories, looking for a social palingenesis that led to the political abandonment of the university, when in fact the university was increasingly becoming a factory, and thus opening up new ambivalences. It was there that they should have looked for new possibilities of a rupture within the social factory.

In his interview in *Futuro anteriore*, Alquati argued that in the early '60s operaismo was tactically based in the factory buildings, focusing its attention and interventions where Taylorism was most rampant, but it was never "*fabbrichista*" (factory-ist), a lover of production and work. The passage from the mass worker to the social worker—to simplify a process that, far from being linear, was full of contradictions, overlaps, and breaks, of discontinuities and continuities—marks the end of this political tactic, which the different groups that we have discussed had trouble finding a replacement for. But "factory-ism" often returned in its ideological dimension, in the nostalgia for manual labor and a continual dystopian re-proposal of the proletarianization of the entire society. What are the new places for the application of the force and exercise of power when the entire society becomes a factory? What is the equivalent of the tactic of the early '60s in relation to the new social subjects? This problem still remains unsolved today.

After the end of operaismo in the strict sense, there were groups that, in a changed context, aimed for a continuity with its method and a discontinuity with its development. Although these attempts had mixed results, and took very different or even opposing paths, there was a general limit that they all shared: Lenin never arrived in England and neither did we move "from spontaneity to spontaneity" as Negri's *Factory of Strategy: 33 Lessons on Lenin* had hypothesized.[31] The organized spontaneity of the workers' struggles of the '60s didn't become the organized spontaneity of the social worker; a suitable organizational form was not found. The social worker continued to be "social" but ceased to be "worker": the subjectivity of a political recomposition didn't oppose itself to the supposed objectivity of the technical composition. Thus, both spontaneity and organization fell into the hands of the enemy. We debated these problems, in different forms, in the forty years that followed.

5 A Dog in a Church: Romano Alquati

Guido Borio

As a political militant, Romano Alquati was a child of his time.[1] We thus have to locate him historically. Born in 1935 in Clana, Istria, he had a comfortable childhood. His father was a general in the fascist army and was killed by the partisans during the days of the insurrection, probably around April 26 or 27, 1945. His body was never recovered. Returning to their roots in the city of Cremona after this family tragedy, the Alquatis fell from being relatively well-off to being isolated and poor, both because of the changed political climate and because they had lost their previous social ties. His mother thus suddenly found herself having to raise him and his two older sisters in poverty.

Alquati's political education was far from linear. In the years immediately following the war, he regularly went to a youth center at which he met people from the Fronte della Gioventù Comunista (Young Communist Front), where he came face to face with the condition of the proletariat. In 1952–1953 he discovered Marx through his association with long-standing militants in Cremona, in a group made up of various communist minorities (councilist, Trotskyist, Bordigist, Luxemburgist, and a few libertarians). They were intergenerational: a few people were older than him, such as Giovanni Bottaioli, an internationalist who had returned from exile in France; and others were his age or only slightly older, such as Danilo Montaldi, and also Renato Rozzi, with whom he developed an important lifelong friendship. Even as a boy Alquati had a keen critical sense, refusing to accept his family's humiliation by the elite, and thus he gave up on his studies in the *liceo classico*[2] to go to a technical school.

The combination of the places he frequented and the local and wider context (the crisis in the Stalinist and third-internationalist positions was beginning to show—it wasn't long before tanks would roll into Budapest) set him off on a course of analysis and research that would guide his future development. Although living in the provinces, he and his young comrades in Cremona started engaging with different rereadings of Marxism, from Italy and abroad. When Alquati and Montaldi went to France they met the Socialisme ou Barbarie group, becoming close to people such as Cornelius Castoriadis, Claude Lefort, and Edgar Morin. They also made links with *Tribune ouvrier* (a workers' newspaper at the Renault factory in which Mothé was an important figure), *Pouvoir ouvrier* in Belgium, *Solidarity for*

Workers' Power in Great Britain, the *Zengakuren* in Japan, *News & Letters* in Chicago, and *Correspondence* in Detroit. This created a kind of informal international network in which they shared experiences with the aim of defining a communist practice, intervention, and position that were critical of, and provided an alternative to, Stalinism. Through this political experience, Alquati and his comrades developed a capacity to reinterpret Marx and Lenin that complemented these other readings.

They had many interests beyond politics, attentively engaging in various emergent critical tendencies, including in literature and art, as well as with new sociological, anthropological, philosophical, and psychoanalytical hypotheses. They also paid close attention to their local context, through the observation and analysis of rural civilization. Alquati's first text, "La festa contadina. Pescarolo: transizione di una situazione agraria" (The country fair: Pescarolo—Transition of an agrarian situation) describes the traditions of a small town near Cremona and was published in 1958 in *Presenza*, a journal of the post-Stalin era. Afterward he analyzed the transformation of agriculture in the Po Valley, showing that farmers had already been subject to a form of "workerization" in the 1800s. The necessity of large-scale agricultural production led to the creation of "green factories," a system in which agriculture overlaps with significant forms of factory-ization aimed at intensive production.

Alquati always presented himself both as a political militant and as a researcher who knew how to use the tools and methodologies of the social sciences. He never specialized in a particular topic, and in fact refused specialization, aware that this was what capitalism required and imposed. He instead aimed at researching issues that linked very different realities, toward finding a possible intrinsic *politicità*. He believed that the militant should understand and indicate the fundamental points and aspects that defined class composition and potential processes of recomposition.

As a result of his experiences in Cremona he joined a local action/inquiry group, called Unità Proletaria, along with Danilo Montaldi, Giovanni Bottaioli, Renato Cavazzini, Gianfranco Fiameni, Stefana Mariotti, and others.

At the end of the 1950s he decided to leave Cremona, first going to Milan—where he got to know the phenomenologists who were students of Enzo Paci, including Giairo Daghini, Nanni Filippini, and Davide Guido Neri—and then to Turin. He refused to become a union official, despite being asked by Pierre Carniti, one of the leaders of CISL.[3] By the end of the '50s he was heavily involved in militant politics and became particularly interested in sociology, which led to exchanges with Alessandro Pizzorno, Roberto Guidicci, Montaldi, and others. Between the end of the 1800s and the beginning of the 1900s, sociology had become fairly important in

Italy through the works of Vilfredo Pareto and Gaetano Mosca. But its rise was interrupted by fascism. After liberation, the PCI disparaged sociology because the communist cadre had been educated in other disciplines, mainly history, philosophy, and economics. Focused on reconstructing their own role, the PSI and the various institutions of the workers' movement had a similar position: they tended to study capitalist development, limiting discourses on the class dimension to ideology. But the rebirth of a certain type of sociology, linked in Italy to the socialist minorities and Catholic intellectuals, led Alquati to study various international texts.

In Turin he met the group of young people linked to Raniero Panzieri who would go on to set up *Quaderni rossi*. Alquati said Panzieri became the journal's "boss." Other acquaintances and friends of Alquati, such as Renato Rozzi, worked for Olivetti's "Center of Psychology," which was an expression of the capitalists' desire to create an intellectuality that supported a certain form of business development based on innovation. The research begun by Alquati is detailed in his articles in *Quaderni rossi* ("Struggle at FIAT" in the first issue and "Organic Composition of Capital and Labor Power at Olivetti," published in two parts in the second and third issues). After splitting from Panzieri, Alquati joined those who would go on to set up *Classe operaia*.

Quaderni rossi is described in historical accounts as a central moment in the rereading of Marx, in particular in its understanding of the relationship between the development of capital, planning, and class. It in fact brought together different positions and points of view: there was the Turin component, led by Panzieri; a Roman component, represented by the young Tronti, Asor Rosa, and others; and then there were other groups like the Venetians and the Genoese. Alquati, together with Gasparotto, Soave, and Gobbi, formed their own group engaged in inquiry-coresearch[4] that interacted with worker militants, differentiating themselves from the others with their heavy focus on what was happening in factories in Turin such as FIAT. Alquati's being a member of *Quaderni rossi*, thus recognizing himself in some of its positions, while at the same time developing his own peculiarities, gave him a certain power in relation to Panzieri and the other groups involved. One of Alquati's fundamental differences was his linking of theoretical construction with research anchored in particular aspects of material reality. In addition to how it is usually remembered, *Quaderni rossi* was an attempt to create an alternative political position, bringing together young militants who were trying to reinterpret theory and organization to adapt them to the new conflicts that were beginning to emerge, along with well-known figures from the socialist party and from Turin's trade unions, such as Vittorio Foa, Sergio Garavini, and Emilio Pugno.

Alquati was already developing his own autonomous critical capacity in that group and was always ready to challenge the positions of others. This was a constant feature of his way of being: creating and maintaining a point of view, concentrating on substance rather than form, not on the group you belong to but on what you propose, a capacity to grasp the elements of weakness and strength in different positions, recognizing the latter and criticizing the former. This meant he could always bring something different to the debate, expressing what others weren't able to see, deepening the collective dimension against individual protagonism. Perhaps this focus on achieving a collective result rather than on being individually dominant was the most important thing about the way he was, the real difference both in his political militancy and in his research. It is an attitude that goes against the grain not only of the institutional Left but also of those groups that would come to be misdescribed as the "new Left." If we analyze the histories of organizers and militants in these circles, we see the repeated return of the affirmation of the individual within the collective, or of small groups within the larger group, at times provoking fractures and splits that didn't have anything to do with substantial differences between their proposals or points of view but were simply based on personal dynamics. Rereading the history of the 1960s and '70s, or what came afterward, you might ask yourself why certain splits happened, and often the only answer is that there were too many roosters in the same coop. This is a problem we still face today.

The second of Alquati's characteristics I'd like to touch on was his capacity to link a strong, intrinsic, and substantial *politicità* with a reading of material reality. This isn't the same as creating a theory to legitimize a point of view; on the contrary, it begins from the hypothesis of reading social reality, class composition, and the contemporary capitalist cycle in order to arrive at a strong political theory. This attitude and method characterized his work throughout his life. Toward the end of the 1950s, he was engaged in analyzing the social urgency expressed by the mass worker in a capitalism focused on the metalwork, chemical, and textile industries. Most people remember Alquati for his work in this period, in which he concentrated more on the class potential of the mass worker than on the movements of capital. I emphasize this because there is a persistent ambiguity at the base of operaismo: despite the fact that there was a radical critique of traditional readings of Marx in the analyses of *Quaderni rossi* and *Classe operaia* in the 1960s, they were often aiming to understand and "valorize" the capitalist dimension rather than to deepen an examination of what was happening within class opposition and of the possible processes of political recomposition. Alquati always politically exalted those who engaged in oppositional behaviors, paying particular attention to struggles and to the working class both as part of the capitalist relationship and, at the same time, as the potential for its rupture and overcoming.

In that period, mainly through his involvement with *Classe operaia*, Alquati completely devoted himself to political militancy, forging relationships with the aim of creating groups for political intervention and research. This differed from his previous experience, for while *Quaderni rossi* aimed at theoretically redefining a relationship with some parts of the union movement and the PSI, *Classe operaia* was born from a desire to politically delink itself from these institutional forms, to become a newspaper of workers' struggles. In the meantime, there had been riots at Piazza Statuto and a renewed conflict in the large factories in Turin, Milan, and Veneto. There seemed to be a search for a new party, as evidenced in Tronti's position in "Lenin in England" on the strategy of the class and the tactics of the party. However, this search came up against some deep-rooted obstacles. First, the group around *Classe operaia* wasn't able to overcome the problem of its limited membership, even if it was anchored in various different situations. And the problem was not only quantitative, but also qualitative: the limits of the previous experience with *Quaderni rossi* remained, including a battle for internal hegemony over the theoretical and organizational line. Some decisions remain incomprehensible, such as that made around the end of 1966 and the beginning of 1967 to disband, leaving the groups that had been formed in an unstable position. And we mustn't forget that Tronti never left the PCI, thus maintaining a deep ambivalence with respect to the party.

Although there were different orientations within *Classe operaia* that entered into dialogue and critical confrontation with each other, they were all completely centered on the figure of the mass worker, attempting to find it a suitable theoretical and organizational form. Alquati contributed with his ability both to read the political composition and to pose the problem of recomposition, as the creation and valorization of the collective subject of opposition. Alquati's proposals were polarizing, though not in order to weave tactical alliances, but as a result of a real attention to a diversity of political hypotheses and theoretical constructions. He had always refused to waver, change, or compromise, and to hold things together that shouldn't be held together, which was the source of the ambiguity typical of these circles. For whereas at the time this ambiguity can seem to be a point of strength, if no real political alternative is created, then everything falls apart afterward. This explains why seemingly strong positions later break down.

In the history of operaismo there are three crucial figures defined by their capacity for analysis, political proposals, and theoretical reasoning: Mario Tronti, Toni Negri, and Romano Alquati. The peculiarities of and differences in their theoretical and militant trajectories and personal attitudes can be summarized as follows: Tronti is characterized by his attention to the *political*, Negri to the *subject*, Alquati to the *process*. What I mean by attention to the process is the capacity to grasp its essence and development, how it is formed and how it can change with time toward opposition, toward another possibility. What is essential is the relationship and the opposition between the two classes—proletariat and capitalists—and how it occurs and develops. This method of reading the process is particularly important for understanding both how capitalism works and how the resubjectivation of the class comes about. If capital and the working class are inseparable, if one is part of the other, then only by negating itself, its own function, can the class become an element of crisis and break the capitalist relation. Alquati often cited Marx's argument that for capital the greatest productive resource was the revolutionary working class, that it is its struggles and opposition that force capitalist subjectivity to redefine itself and develop. So, from an antagonistic and revolutionary point of view, the most significant aspect to consider is the process—in terms both of the alterity of the working class and of the capitalist tendency that must be intercepted and blocked—because it can characterize and provide the basis for theory, analysis, and political research. It allows us to understand what is changed and what is created.

Those who met Alquati often describe him as having been a solitary person, even unfriendly. I think this is a misperception. He was always very good at engaging not only with people who agreed with his point of view but also with those who had different positions. He never passed judgment a priori, in an ideological way. He always developed critiques or deepened points of agreement in order to get to the substance of the matter, considering what was useful for reinforcing and enriching hypotheses and explaining why he thought other things should be abandoned if inadequate or useless to the construction of a partisan point of view. Alquati always embraced people and situations with the desire to develop their potential through a process of enrichment, encouraging them to see that what already existed wasn't enough, to move toward the construction of a powerful alternative. He insisted on the cultivation of subjectivity, understood as the growth and transformation of both individual and collective capacities and possibilities.

Alquati always insisted that intrinsic *politicità* had its origins in the social. Politics was not a separate dimension (as was held by those who believed in the autonomy of the political). He focused particularly on strengthening the unity of the class as a force of opposition. He thus gave substance to his political proposal by subordinating it to the material situation. He created a theory and proposal for political action that wasn't founded in separateness, but began from that which, in the specific situation, could have strength in a process of the accumulation and valorization of opposition. His was an attitude and method that based the creation of theory on the necessity of political action. But his research was always hypothetical; his proposals, elaborations, and analyses were never given definitively. Even when he came to conclusions, they always served as the basis for another leap forward.

This is a good way of looking at things, because certainties are refused a priori. It runs contrary to the way in which political analysis and political proposals are often used, as a tool to compete with other individuals or groups. Even when you are competing with the enemy class, if you don't have the capacity to go further, to increase your power in the long term, you soon find yourself in a position of weakness. The theoretical weapons and the practical organizational forms we have to create are always provisional. Some are taken from the enemy and others are built by us, but they are never definitive. Alquati hypothesized a process of collective liberation from capitalist civilization, a process of rupture able to accumulate power rather than simply engage in self-representation.

This was another of his characteristics, his capacity to keep looking ahead, to grasp the possibilities to come and not simply to consolidate that which already existed. It was the construction of a theoretical, organizational, and political force. These are significant elements that mean that not only the context but also our way of being have to be put into play. In each new context we have to start again in order to strengthen what we are, as much at the level of the vanguard as at the level of the class.

Alquati shared and re-proposed Marx's method for the construction of forms of abstraction: starting from concrete reality, defining or hypothesizing the foundational and substantial category variables of a process, and then trying to understand how the identified and chosen categories relate to each other. He first created a static description of a social phenomenon, tracing its fundamental characteristics, then he considered the influence and peculiarities of the other subvariables, and afterward he proposed a model indicating the interrelations between these categories. Once the hypothesis was defined, it was located within the process, thus proceeding from a static to a dynamic dimension, as from a photograph to a film. Then, in the next passage of analysis the focus was on movement, considering all the possible changes between and within categories in the development of a phenomenon. Thus, there is an attempt to understand the changes in the links and interconnections, relationships and forces, in order to arrive at an initial synthesis. And then the spiral of analysis begins again. I realize that this could sound like a mere description of the methodology used for any research aimed at a specific goal. But it is much more than that, as there is a substantial political difference: the construction of knowledge for a partisan aim. What characterizes this process is the object of the coresearch, why it is being done, and for what ends. As I have already outlined, this type of action is always aimed at a possible future rupture, at what could happen, at the relationship between reality and possibility.

After his participation in *Classe operaia*, Alquati didn't have a militant role in other political organizations, neither in the 1970s nor afterward. However, he continued to be politically militant and retained his specific *politicità* in relation to social reality, never giving up the search for a relationship with what emerged implicitly in the class, both as an enlarged subjectivity and as a conflictual insurgence.

He carried out research and politics for about fifty years in formal and informal groups, as a point of reference for others, including and educating hundreds of people who engaged with him and his research. He created and shared a wealth of thought without demanding influence, without ever asking for anything in return, if not the satisfaction of having understood the fundamentals of current-day capitalist civilization much better than others, and therefore of being able to express a well-founded and substantial refusal of it.

Alquati found himself facing a rapidly changing situation. He was always very good at anticipating capitalist transformation, mutations within class composition, changes in work, science, knowledge, education, communication, and so on. His hypotheses were developed through research into the factory, the university, the service sector, the tertiary sector, the family, health, artificial intelligence (already at the beginning of the 1980s), and the human capacity of reproduction.[5]

The second part of this chapter shows how Alquati saw the relationship between politics and research as unbreakable and of utmost importance:[6] in order to define, practice, or sustain an antagonistic action, politics and research couldn't be separate but had to grow and develop together, reinforcing each other. To understand this, we must look at the link between these two moments, which is given by the fact that intrinsic *politicità* has its origins in the social, and coresearch is a process that activates and organizes social subjects so that they are able to autonomously create knowledge and methods for the development of counter-subjectivity. This is why considering these dynamics as interdependent rather than separate is so important for Alquati. We must always ask ourselves what processes are happening, how they work, and what outcomes they lead to. This is the aim of the political militant, to seek out the possibility of conflict that could be given or is already given in the class, intensifying it toward the construction of a partisan point of view. For Alquati, the party is nothing other than that which elaborates, develops, and strengthens political theory, which takes on an organizational form aimed at strengthening and giving perspective to the actions and intrinsic *politicità* of the class. This continual back and forth creates a theoretical proposal for research that is suitable for reading the complexity of social reality, because it has a specific vision that pushes mobilized and recomposed collective subjectivities toward identifying and creating wider, longer-lasting, and more politically powerful moments of conflict and rupture. The form of the party is transitory and changing, and is tasked with strengthening the class, proposing informal but substantial forms of self-organization in order to create greater possibilities of rupture. Relationships of force and recomposition are created in this to-and-fro of theory and practice.

Of course, political research gives power to political praxis, but research is also a response to a political goal. Thus that which defines the political and *politicità* cannot be separated from reality or overdetermine it. *Politicità* exists when you are able to read and divert the tendency of capitalist development. This is another crucial point for Alquati. Today the political is completely delinked from research; research is done by technicians with the aim of giving the institutional political system more up-to-date tools for reinforcing its systemic domination. Institutional politics makes use of technical skills created by research, which are simply aimed at sustaining a certain political position. In Alquati the organizational form is not an end or a function in itself but provides the possibility for advancing a project. You can take the most functional and powerful organizational form that already exists and bend it and guide it toward a political end.

In Alquati's model of capitalism, the function of domination is on a higher level than other functions such as accumulation, the valorization process, daily life, and social behavior. His model is capable of grasping the differences between these levels of capitalist reality, which are organized hierarchically and include domination, accumulation, valorization, the production of useful activities, and then other lower levels. Alquati had a particular ability to read these different levels and see what differed within them, leading him to criticize other political analyses that failed to take them into account. He always maintained that this was the most powerful method of abstraction and reasoning. In a situation of antagonism and opposition, the capacity to strengthen theory, reasoning, research, and inquiry is fundamental for guiding and empowering praxis, which then, defining itself, in turn supplies new elements necessary for redefining a deeper and more up-to-date knowledge.

To look more closely at these categories, let's return to two aspects of Alquati's method and attitude. The first was to consider the specific aspects of *ambivalence*, something that he adapts from Marx. We must be able to see differences—elements that go in different and opposite directions—within a phenomenon, such as that in Marx's famous reading of the commodity's use value (the usefulness of the specific commodity) and exchange value (how it enters into the valorization process and the production of surplus value). Think also of constant capital and variable capital, dead labor and living labor, which are counterposed in a single relationship. Alquati re-elaborates this capacity to read substantial differences within a category or a phenomenon, proposing them as the possibility for an alternative. If you look carefully, the double character of the commodity as use value and exchange value also indicates a substantial alternative between a specific utility and a capitalist utility; the negation of the capitalist relationship is in the negation of the commodity, above all when the commodity is human capacity itself. Therefore, we need to be able to grasp the differences that define an ambivalence: a phenomenon is given in a certain way but could have another tendency. Valorizing one aspect of ambivalence is what enriches a process, against that aspect of it that supports what is hostile to us.

Alquati's discourse on the *unresolved residue* is also important. Reality and social relations are never completely new; there is always something left over from a previous situation whose possibilities we can influence. Capitalist society is the result of a process containing the remainder of previous elements and perspectives that could develop differently. We must therefore identify the times and forms in which they evolve and are transformed. Alquati always pointed to the persistence of different situations, because it was that which made it possible to aim at transformation. This is vital when we are thinking about capitalist subsumption and reproduction, and also about rupture and a possible way out.

Now let's look at some categories and variables that the late Alquati began developing in the 1980s in his reading of hyper-industrial society. His *modellone* (literally, "the big model")[7] proposed a way of interpreting the reality of contemporary capitalism. Some of its most important themes include *formazione*, *communication*, *science*, *subjectivity*, and the *reproduction of human capacity*. Alquati proposes his analysis within a theory of the *medium range*—the capacity to locate oneself and to embed research in the bridge between the high levels of abstraction and the levels of reality below. I have chosen these categories because, in his discourse on militancy and political action, Alquati poses the question of *barycentrality*, that is, of where the political militant is located not only individually but also organizationally. Obviously, political and militant action permeate all the social fields of life and relationships, but they should be situated in a place in capitalist reality where, in that specific moment, there is the possibility of influencing the relations of force. Here, political action has a substantial possibility for rupture precisely because it is based on the capacity to choose the moments of strength, and not weakness, in the development of the capitalist dimension. The choice on which operaismo was founded was to search for conflict, opposition, otherness, and autonomy at the highest levels of capitalism.

For Alquati, *formazione*[8] is a process of modifying and strengthening the capacity of the human subject.[9] It is a particular capitalist necessity, allowing the subject to engage in a process of accumulating skills acquired at their own expense (allowing the capitalist to save), in order to better produce things for others and thus in order to best be exploited. *Formazione* is one of the most substantial necessities/interests of capitalism in its passage to hyper-industrial society. It is a process of subtraction and separation that affects the proletariat, simultaneously strengthening it and depriving it of possibilities. In peasant society and also in classic industrial society, *formazione* is above all determined by how the family, the environment, and work define people and their subjectivity. In those phases, therefore, the productive process used a *formazione* that already existed. Since then, capitalism has industrialized *formazione*, turning it into work: it defines the capacities, skills, and attitudes that the subject has to have and how and where they should acquire them. To reach this objective the school and university become specifically industrialized environments.[10] But *formazione* also happens in wider and less easily recognizable contexts, such as in the use and consumption of particular commodities—lifestyles, entertainment, information, and performance. But within these fields, precisely because they are fundamental to the process of accumulation, there could be a counter-*formazione*, an activity aimed at ends opposed to those of capitalism. Locating oneself there, in these factories of industrialized *formazione*, and acting in opposition, toward recomposition, therefore means weakening or stopping the capitalist process. *Formazione*, as the word itself implies, "forms," modifies, that is, transmits and constructs capacities that then, in their ambivalence, are exploited and turned toward capitalist necessities, but that could also be turned against them.

At the beginning of the 1990s in particular, Alquati analyzes the role of communication[11] (in Turin there were also discussions and analyses linked to the establishment of an alternative local radio). Communication is part of a level that lies below that of *formazione*. It consists in the circulation of information and knowledge in formal or informal organizational networks, which are treated almost always as commodities and activate other productive processes that already exist. Instead, *formazione* is the constitution of something that doesn't exist yet. However, communication is powerful, because it supports an organizational form.

In the 1970s Alquati had already begun to reflect on science and technology as elements empowering the capitalist dimension, a line of research that he continued in the 1980s. Science is above all Galilean science, created in factories and aimed at supporting the necessities of the system and current civilization.[12] Science empowers and optimizes human capacities, reproducing them by modifying them, extending them, and socializing them, in order to appropriate them and transfer them into the capitalist machinery, including into its organization. Underlying this are new relations of force that produce new asymmetries and make the idea of proposing another science seem difficult, despite all the philosophical and epistemological attempts that have been made. Science has always been tightly linked to and defined by the requirements of systemic domination, and to the processes of the production, accumulation, and valorization of capital. Alquati fights a long battle on the fields of science, knowledge, and possible forms of art and creativity, maintaining that the Left divides commodities into good and bad, while in reality science, knowledge, and art are also commodities, and are contained inside the commodification process. He therefore rejects this division between good commodities (science, knowledge, art, etc.) and bad commodities (tangible goods such as cars, etc.). There is even an ideology in which culture is not a commodity, but a noble entity. In fact, culture is a commodity with a specific function; it is a terrain for the production and valorization of capital. Alquati's research in the 1970s and in *Università di ceto medio*[13] showed that culture and knowledge were produced and reproduced as commodities to be incorporated within a new intellectual proletariat, with the function of strengthening the processes of industrialization that were already underway.

Commodity above all means separation from the living body of the proletariat that produces it. The distinctive thing about the commodity is its being produced to be sold, used, and possessed by someone else, in this case by capitalist cooperation. In the same way, the potential wealth of knowledge and science is not for those who produce and embody it but is destined for other ends. Marx discussed this in relation to alienation. Alquati deepened and developed the question of separateness, which is what allows knowledge and science to be appropriated by the capitalist system. The power of knowledge and science is therefore used to the benefit not of the class[14] but of whoever uses it in the processes of valorization. On this basis, Alquati analyzes the significance of the industrialization of science in its relationship with technology and develops and deepens a substantial analysis of past human activity incorporated in machinery.

Science today is perhaps the principal means for the construction of other and more powerful organizational apparatuses, founded also and above all on the informatization of processes and commodities. It is therefore always generated for capitalist industrialization and valorization. Technology is the application of science within determinate processes. Science is therefore a specific commodity; it is that which today—together with human capacity—creates most valorization. Science and technology strengthen human action and work. In Taylorism, science had a certain rigidity: it was broken down into tasks and functions. Now the flexibilization of productive processes has created a strengthening of science and knowledge, always with the macro-goal of the accumulation of domination.

Therefore, Alquati warns, science is not simply that which we understand it to be in lay terms, namely, the scientific disciplines (physics, math, biology, etc.); the most powerful science is social science, because it allows for the strengthening of the function of society and for the redefinition of the form of domination. Within the capitalist process, some tertiary sectors, and sectors linked to new technologies, become fundamental, for instance, the services, school, *formazione*, and health. In neo-modernity, reproduction has become the central sphere of capitalist valorization. Here we can see Alquati's major battle to understand the past and future development of capitalist civilization, unlike those who identified production as happening exclusively in the secondary sector, or rather in the production of tangible goods, or those who saw in the general intellect only new immaterial production. Taking his cue from thinkers such as Claudio Napoleoni, Alquati maintained the centrality of social valorization. Capitalist subjectivity is also productive, in opposition to us and to the alterity that we represent.

Alquati's way of posing himself as critical and different meant he became very isolated. He had to conduct a theoretical battle with the ruling Left in the 1980s and 1990s, who were anchored in the ideology of the valorization of supposedly neutral or not even capitalist "good" commodities. While capital used the commodity to valorize and construct its domination, those who should have opposed it instead pushed for the development of the commodities that were supposedly good or neutral, losing sight of the daily negativity of capitalist civilization. Even before the economic subordination of the Left in its various forms, we find a subordination of its thought and theory. At the end of the 1980s Alquati published two books on his model of the functioning of the capitalist system.[15] Afterward he redefined his reasoning and hypothesis in another unpublished text, "Nella società industriale d'oggi" (In today's industrial society).

Alquati was never a positivist or a follower of scientism, and never believed in a work ethic like those of the left socialist tradition. In his studies on labor, he rejected the discourse on the cognitariat, which was proposed by Negri and others in the 1990s, producing a very different analysis. Commodities, as we were saying, can't be divided into good and bad. However, there are commodities that, in their ambivalence, contain greater possibilities of being counter-used in processes of decommodification. Beyond the specific utility that makes up the particular character of each commodity—a pen, a recording device, a computer, a mobile telephone—a theatrical performance or a book are not so different from a washing machine or a car, especially as today everything is combined and governed by communicative networks (think, for example, of the smart home). Only the commodity understood as a capacity contained in people has a specific ambivalence. The way out from capitalism is through the possibility of breaking this process of separation. Therefore a discourse on human capacity is fundamental to breaking with the tendency of capitalist development. The central industriality is located no longer in particular buildings, but within the new social factories. This is why, through analyzing the processes of the commodification of human capacity and acting to counter them, we could build a force of opposition to capitalist development.

Alquati then describes what this commodity of human capacity is,[16] pointing out that it is not simply material participation in production, because faculties and skills that are emotional and psychological are also involved. What becomes sellable and valorizable (here Alquati is heavily indebted to Jean Baudrillard) are specific signs and characteristics, more than the tangible object in itself. Thus, knowledge is supported by the human as such. The cycles of capitalist accumulation increasingly invest in people as having a capacity that needs to be reproduced and modified. This is suggested, for example, in the development of industrialized medicine, with its applied research on the genome and the possibility of intervening in the human body. Alquati's discourse is substantially different from those that became mainstream. By analyzing how capitalism develops and what spaces the current capitalist system of valorization, exploitation, and separation opens up, he puts forward a very important hypothesis.[17]

Alquati also extensively focuses on labor and activity in his notes, some of which were published.[18] He challenges arguments about the end of work that were popular in the late 1990s (such as those held by Jeremy Rifkin and André Gorz). Labor, he tells us, has a strictly capitalist character and defines a way of being in the civilization in which we are situated. Activity is different, as it defines human necessities. Activity is generic, labor is specific. Just as capitalism didn't exist for most of human history and therefore could cease to exist, the same can be said of labor. But humans can't fail to engage in activity. Alquati also responds to some vulgarizations of the idea of the refusal of labor: it does not simply mean not working, but subtracting oneself from the capitalist relationship and from the particular needs that capitalism imposes on proletarians with the commodification of their capacity. Activity is, on the contrary, the valorization and satisfaction of the human person. Labor makes us actors, created for and acting for someone else, while *activity* is created for ourselves, not only as individuals but as a collective.

Here the question of the unresolved residue returns. The capitalist tendency aims at modifying activity by turning it into labor, industrializing and separating human capacity as a commodity. But this tendency is not fully realizable for capitalism. The current debate, in which it is held that all labor will become automated, is an ideological rather than a real proposition. There will be parts that become automated, but other parts that cannot be. For example, relational, caring, and reproductive labor, almost always the work of women,[19] and also labor that exercises social control (today there is little understanding of how much these two types of labor overlap and complement each other) cannot be automated, even though they are now organized industrially and can make use of some technologies, largely, but not only, of an organizational kind. Labor defines the capitalist relation: if you abolish labor you would abolish capitalism itself. It is not a question of philosophical dialectics: given that the accumulation of domination and value requires the commodification of human capacity, by abolishing labor you would abolish the possibility of the capitalist class accumulating domination and value.

Finally, Alquati always insisted on subjectivity. He was frustrated that his attempts to bring the problem of subjectivity to his collective political experiences were repeatedly refused. From *Quaderni rossi* and *Classe operaia* onward, no one wanted to deal with it. He didn't carry out any specific research on subjectivity, because it implicitly permeated all of his research.

The subject can be capitalist, or it can be the counter-subjectivity of a hyper-proletariat that wants to escape capitalism. In the process of creating counter-subjectivity we go beyond the dimension of the actor. Counter-subjectivity is the capacity to represent ourselves and act for ourselves, in a relation of opposition. Capitalist subjectivity is about being able to dominate; the counter-subjectivity of the class is characterized by being able to break this relationship of domination and construct an alternative, an otherness, an autonomy. Autonomy, for Alquati, is always a relationship with something else, the construction of a collective force. Intrinsic *politicità* is the capacity to modify the relations of force. And in capitalist society the litmus test of these relations is the wage.

Some final words on autonomy: it's not about living in a bubble separated from everything else, but about acting in a specific way and putting real opposition into action. You thus construct yourself as an alternative to and different from something else. If we look at revolutionary processes, we see that it is precisely the incapacity to go beyond a certain limit that leads to their decline. So, antagonism is positioning oneself in opposition; autonomy is constructing a diversity that depends on what there is but at the same time is able to construct something that doesn't exist yet. The liberation from capitalism is not a messianic ideology in which communism would be the solution to everything. There would also be contradictions to be faced in a non-capitalist society, as there were before capitalism existed. Take the relationship between human beings and nature: human beings are part of nature, and so, in the development of subjective action, have to come into conflict with nature. Green ideology often doesn't consider the capitalist dimension, and therefore ignores class relations and processes of commodification. Ecology today already presupposes a new form of industrialization. And even in the liberation from capitalism, the contradictions in both the conflictual relationship between human beings and the relationship between human beings and nature will remain; we will still come up against limits, but they will assume new forms.

For Alquati, the liberation from capitalism presupposes the capacity to imagine and hypothesize a subjectivity able to break with the process of commodification. This is the strategic revolutionary dimension; it is no longer that of the separateness of the political. Yet there remains an unsolved problem. Subjectivity has an individual value, but also an organizational collective dimension, which for Alquati always raises the question of the party. But we should be careful here: we are talking of the party as a form, not in the way it is normally understood. The party is a point of view that represents a difference. There is thus a capitalist subjectivity that supports a project and realizes a process, and there could be a counter-subjectivity that defines a project of opposition to and liberation from capitalist civilization, and that is realized in a process of struggles and successive ruptures, increasingly founded on the capacity to negate the space and perspective of the enemy. At the moment, capitalist civilization is what there is and what is predominant. This is a macro-opposition—in the sense of two opposing classes, which contain smaller groups—in which there is a relationship between class composition and political elites. In his interview in *Futuro anteriore*, Alquati identifies the wealth and above all the limits of subjectivity within the processes of realized or failed revolutionary transformations and ruptures in different historical periods around problems that still remain decisive today.

I am aware of the insufficiencies of this brief exposition, which doesn't do justice to Alquati. I would like to end by saying that he was always a "dog in a church," not only in the university but wherever he found himself, also among his many "comrades," not to mention the Italian intellectuals. He was always being a nuisance and for this reason his thought was almost always ignored, but then being a nuisance is perhaps the most important quality of revolutionary subjectivity.

6 Returning to First Principles

What is left of operaismo after the defeat of the mass worker and the premature abortion of the autonomous development of the "social worker"? For some, nothing. For others, "post-operaismo." For us, a method and style. In the previous chapters we have sketched out this position, which we will now summarize, one step at a time.

The different political paths of the operaist constellation diverged or even entered into conflict in the 1970s, finally seeming to implode in the 1980s. In the desert of capitalist counter-revolution, the collective dimension of operaismo was subject to increasing individualization and fragmentation, marked by the different personal choices of those involved and, in some cases, by time spent in prison, as well as by conflicts over internal decisions. It should be clear at this point in the book that when we say "capitalist counter-revolution" we are not talking about a mere restructuring within the logic and needs of the dominant system. We mean a process that responds to the revolutionary process of a determinate class composition, to break it, fragment it, depoliticize it, and transform it into a productive resource in order to allow the system to leap forward. The capitalist counter-revolution is the transformation of revolution into innovation, into a process of profound change on the medium and base levels of the system, leaving the high levels of the accumulation of domination and capital unchanged.

In terms of the transmission of militant consciousness, the 1980s and 1990s seem like a black hole: very little was written about them, as if nothing or next to nothing happened beyond rampant capitalist restructuring. But there were paths below the desert sands, attempting to maintain continuity with the 1970s and its political experiences and struggles. This is the real "Italian anomaly," with its history of organizational processes that, with interruptions, impasses, and various limits, continues to the present day. Without these lines of continuity and discontinuity, it's impossible to understand the struggles in Italy against nuclear power stations and American military bases in the 1980s, or the experiences of the occupied social centers of the 1990s. Although there is a tendency to think that nothing happened between April 7, 1977, and Genoa 2001, we must fill this apparent vacuum with analysis: not for historiographical reasons but because, in order to look ahead, it is politically necessary to begin from the wealth and the limits of what lies behind us, in our history.

Sentimenti dell'aldiqua (Sentiments of this world) was published in 1990, the product of a collective reflection aimed at a radical critique of the "weak thought" of postmodernism.[1] The authors included various figures that took part in the experiences of the operaist constellation, including Piperno, Virno, Berti, and Lucio Castellano. Giorgio Agamben, a philosopher who would later gain international recognition, took part in the preparatory discussions, as well as Marco Bascetta, a journalist from the Italian newspaper *Il manifesto*, on whose culture pages a few comrades linked to the operaist experience had tried to carve out a space for themselves. Its subtitle, "Opportunismo paura cinismo nell'età del disincanto" (Opportunism fear cynicism in the age of disillusionment), indicated the sentiments considered in the book, all typical of that age. The aim of the book was to subvert the Left's interpretation of these sentiments, opening them up to ambivalence, trying to read in them not only the extreme individualism prevalent in the 1980s but also the possibility of new forms of conflict in unlikely places of production, and to do this with neither nostalgia for the past nor resignation to the present. The book concludes with Rossana Rossanda's response to its arguments, in which she makes a reasonable critique of its excessive illusions, but also reproduces a certain left nostalgia for times past. We would say, rather, that the book's method was correct, but its conclusions were inadequate, remaining stuck at the level of philosophical abstraction.

Coming out of the discussion group that followed *Sentimenti dell'aldiqua*, *Luogo comune* (Commonplace/Place-in-common) was founded. It was one of the journals that would lay the ground for the debates of the 1990s. Others followed, including *DeriveApprodi* (the longest-lasting, most diverse, and probably most important), *Altreragioni* (in which Bologna and Gambino initially took part), and, in the following decade, *Posse*, to which Negri was central. And we mustn't forget the French *Futur antérieur*, founded in 1990 as a result of the relationship between Negri and the Trotskyist Jean-Marie Vincent, and later, *Multitudes*, to which Yann Moulier-Boutang contributed.

The context had changed since the '60s and '70s, and so too had the function of journals. Now they were used for the elaboration, and, in some cases, systematization, of theoretical discourse, but no longer for political organization. Or where they were, it was in rather traditional ways, through the outsourcing of theory: entrusting intellectuals with the task of producing a discourse separate from practice able to create a so-called imaginary through its "mythopoeia" of abstract suggestions and captivating concepts. The organic intellectual had returned on a smaller scale, more as farce than as tragedy.

In some of these journals the concepts and categories were forged that would later become commonplace in so-called post-operaismo (this term, coined in Anglo-Saxon academia, should—taking Tronti's words out of context—be met with nothing less than physical violence!). Among others, these concepts and categories included the general intellect, production and language, immaterial labor, exodus, and multitude. These theorizations took place in the context of a profound change in the forms of production summarized under the category of "post-Fordism," which was developed in discussion with the French regulation school (which included people such as Michele Aglietta, Robert Boyer, and Benjamin Coriat).

We will now make a few points about these interpretative instruments. The first regards the context defined as "post-Fordist." We have already seen that Fordism and Taylorism are two distinct terms that in a determinate historical period enter into a close relationship, laying out the coordinates between factory and society within which the forms of labor and life, exploitation and struggle, are determined. But the distinction between them often becomes confused: the calling into question of the Taylorist regime of the factory tends to be interpreted as an overcoming of Fordism, going beyond Fordism's logic of social organization around the connection between production and consumption. Alquati claimed that while the category of "post-Fordism" implies a rupture in the system of capital's regulation, this period actually saw an expansion of the social factory, and thus continuity in the change. Criticizing both the nostalgia of "past-ism" and the illusions of "new-ism," he called it "hyper-Fordism" and proposed a different reading of what he termed "hyper-industrialization."

Our second point regards the general intellect, a concept that is taken from Marx's *Grundrisse*, which brought together a number of manuscripts and notebooks that had lain unpublished for many years. First published between 1939 and 1941 by the Marx-Engels-Lenin Institute in Moscow, the Italian version came out between 1968 and 1970 in two volumes, and was translated by Enzo Grillo, a comrade who had played an active role in the experience of *Quaderni rossi* and *Classe operaia* and was later involved in Potere Operaio.[2]

The concept of the general intellect is found in the *Grundrisse* in the "Fragment on Machines" in which Marx identifies "[t]he increase of the productive force of labour and the greatest possible negation of necessary labour" as "the necessary tendency of capital."[3] There is a "transformation of the means of labour into machinery, and of living labour into a mere living accessory of this machinery, as the means of its action."[4] In the productive process, the means of labor undergo diverse metamorphoses, the last of which is "an automatic system of machinery . . . set in motion by an automaton, a moving power that moves itself; this automaton consisting of numerous mechanical and intellectual organs, so that the workers themselves are cast merely as its conscious linkages."[5] This automatic system of machines represents the maximum development of fixed capital, that is, of objective scientific capacity, which "indicates to what degree general social knowledge has become a direct force of production, and to what degree, hence, the conditions of the process of social life itself have come under the control of the general intellect and been transformed in accordance with it. To what degree the powers of social production have been produced, not only in the form of knowledge, but also as immediate organs of social practice, of the real life process."[6]

As Bifo has often pointed out, if we look more closely at these passages we can see that there is almost no subjective tension here. Marx describes a necessary tendency in the development of fixed capital and of the automatic system of machines in which the general intellect is objectified, whereby capital works toward its own dissolution. Or rather, "to the degree that large industry develops, the creation of real wealth comes to depend less on labour time and on the amount of labour employed than on the power of the agencies set in motion during labour time, whose 'powerful effectiveness' is itself in turn out of all proportion to the direct labour time spent on their production, but depends rather on the general state of science and on the progress of technology, or the application of this science to production."[7]

We can see the relationship between Marx's reflections here and Alquati's analysis of the social knowledge incorporated in living labor, which was taken up again in the early 2000s under the category of "living knowledge."

The development process is set in motion by the antagonism of the social relation, from an open conflict between the autonomy of living labor and the objectification of social knowledge. The victorious side in this relationship of force determines the development of the general intellect in one direction or another. Thus, there is no "necessary" tendency but only *possible* and conflicting tendencies. From the perspective of those who aim to break from capitalism there can be no illusory overcoming, but only a search for rupture.

In the analyses of the 1990s, the concept of the general intellect returned to its supposed necessary tendency: capitalist development created its own overcoming. The general intellect seemed to be subjectivized in these analyses, embodied in so-called immaterial laborers or in the indefinite "multitude," but in fact it became even more objectified, because these subjects were considered in their abstractness, or rather, not in their concrete behavior and possibilities for conflict, in their subjectivity, but, on the contrary, in their mere existence within the technical composition of capital. The abstraction became indeterminate, and the signs of conflict within the process were lost. It was argued that social cooperation was central to the new forms of production without questioning what this social cooperation was, how it behaved, how it was subjectivized, and what ends it acted for. And as social cooperation was central for capital, it *immediately* had political centrality on our side. The very notion of "immediateness" is problematic, as actually the process is continuously mediated by relationships of exploitation, force, and conflict. Thus, as we said above, there is no necessary overcoming, but only the possibility of rupture. However, in these theorizations rupture was often subsumed by necessity, concrete subjectivity by a masked objectivity, the potential of antagonistic cooperation by the glorification of cooperation in the labor process. Capital, as Negri repeatedly stressed in the 1990s, had become a simple parasitic shell over a cooperation that was already free and autonomous, as if liberty and autonomy were given by the development of capital rather than by the development of conflict, by labor rather than by struggles against labor; as if subjectivity wasn't itself an outcome of production, and therefore the field of a potential clash between the forces of capital and the (real or potential) forces of antagonism; as if technical composition was again immediately translatable into political composition, exactly as it had been in traditional Marxism and in the socialist and communist parties. It seemed that the concepts of autonomy, subjectivity, and class composition—mainstays of the operaist method—had disappeared, emphasized and repeated only in their disembodied abstractness.

From this perspective we can also see—and this is our third point—the differences that, beginning from a common operaist matrix, unfolded in relation to the method of the tendency and the question of temporality. The concept of tendency is a question of anticipation and of making a political wager: to anticipate the possibilities on your side for interrupting, deviating, and overturning the development of the other side; to wager politically on the potential forces through which to bring about processes of recomposition. This is the reason why the operaisti took up Marx's work and followed Lenin's initiative: to move forward. To do this, Tronti writes in *Workers and Capital*, we need to simultaneously anticipate and follow:

Anticipating means thinking, seeing many things in one, seeing them in development, watching everything with theoretical eyes and from the point of view of our own class. *Following* means acting, moving at the real level of social relations, measuring the material state of the present forces, grasping the moment in the here and now to snatch the initiative in the struggle.... In certain moments, the possibility of getting a sense of the struggle—and of organisation—lies exactly in the ability to foresee capital's objective path and its needs within the terms of this path. We must thwart the fulfilment of these necessities and thus block capital's development, pitching it into crisis before—sometimes long before—it has achieved the ideal conditions that we have ourselves contemplated.[8]

And:

It can never be repeated enough that to foresee capital's development does not mean submitting to its iron laws: rather, it means forcing it to take a certain road, waiting in ambush at some point with weapons more powerful than iron, where we can attack and smash it.[9]

This is the tendency: to understand where the enemy is going, to stop them, to lay in ambush for them at a point in which we are strong and they are weak; to grasp hold of development, in order to interrupt it and turn it in a different direction. Otherwise the concept of tendency will either become something like a horoscope for the future or will offer up solutions to the enemy.

In Negri, and in some of so-called post-operaismo, the tendency often ends up getting reidentified with necessity, the revolutionary process with teleology. This is taken to the point of accelerationism, in which the more capital develops, the more the autonomy of living labor develops. The problem of the rupture disappears, innovation devours revolution, and after this 360-degree turn, we are back to where we started: Marxist determinism, dressed up as an abstract and disembodied subjectivity that is given different names at different times. It has to be said that this result isn't totally at odds with its operaist origins; operaismo did show some ambiguity with respect to development. But here the necessity of being within development destroys any attempt at being against it. However, other positions that we have detailed above showed different possibilities, completely at odds with this evolutionist glorification of History.

For a final consideration of the old question of the law of value, let's return to "The Fragment on Machines":

> To the degree that labour time—the mere quantity of labour—is posited by capital as the sole determinant element, to that degree does direct labour and its quantity disappear as the determinant principle of production—of the creation of use values—and is reduced both quantitatively, to a smaller proportion, and qualitatively, as an, of course, indispensable but subordinate moment, compared to general scientific labour, technological application of natural sciences, on one side, and to the general productive force arising from social combination [*Gliederung*] in total production on the other side—a combination which appears as a natural fruit of social labour (although it is a historic product).[10]

Here we find capital working toward its own destruction as the dominant form of production.

Presupposing the necessity of this tendency, the end of the law of value is declared in a rather unproductive debate with those who claimed its complete continuity. Both positions are mistaken because they are built on the same basis: the idea that the measure of labor depends on the objectivity of the forms of production. In fact, this measure isn't at all objective; it depends on the relations of force between the classes; it is—as we have seen with the wage—the spoils of war in the fight between workers and capital. It is what is at stake in a political conflict.

Moreover, Marx himself, a few pages after setting out the necessary tendency toward capital's dissolution, lets in by the back door what he'd let out at the front: "Capital itself is the moving contradiction, [in] that it presses to reduce labour time to a minimum, while it posits labour time, on the other side, as sole measure and source of wealth. Hence it diminishes labour time in the necessary form so as to increase it in the superfluous form; hence posits the superfluous in growing measure as a condition—question of life or death—for the necessary."[11] Therefore, imposing its own measure is a question of life or death for capital. And as long as there isn't a force able to threaten capital with death, it will continue to live by imposing measure. When today people make appeals to the conscience of so-called civil society against the immorality of unpaid labor, arguing that work should always be paid, they are wrong. If the bosses have enough control over the relations of force to make the proletariat work without paying them, then they will do so without hesitation. In the same way, redistribution doesn't depend on any logical necessity within capital. The only logic is political: the class war, whether real or potential.

Those who tried to rethink the legacy of operaismo at the end of the 1980s were moved by the right intentions; that is, they wanted to overturn the narrative of the *pensée unique* of "neoliberalism" (a term that ends up sweetening capitalism, making it secondary); they wanted to identify new potentialities for conflict in a context in which the relations of force were tipped strongly in favor of the enemy. However, this justified attack on any nostalgic form often ended up being pretty ideological, leaving the materiality of social relations behind in order to shelter in the heavens of hypothesis.[12]

To give a concrete example, in our reading of the transformation of work at the turn of the millennium, we preferred to speak about the "cognitivization of work" rather than "cognitive work" (let's leave aside the horrible oxymoron "immaterial labor"). This is not simply a linguistic question, but indicates a different approach, which was particularly useful in political movements by university students (in the last thirty years, the university was perhaps the most significant social context in which this theoretical debate was applied politically). Cognitivization is a process of the organization and hierarchization of the forms of production and exploitation in a phase in which knowledge becomes increasingly central to capital accumulation. Using the term "cognitive labor" as if it were an already given subject often ended up slipping into defining workers in a sectorial sense, or rather, into counterposing manual workers and intellectual workers, or into again seeing the most advanced point of technical composition ("knowledge workers") as the most advanced point of struggle. But any idea of a progressive linearity must be resisted: the cognitivization of work also means the cognitivization of exploitation and measure, of hierarchy and tasks. The subject does not precede the process, and neither is it a necessary result of it. The subject is formed in and against the process, where it is able to call into question and interrupt the line of capitalist development.

It goes without saying that cognitivization, like other categories, must be radically problematized and called into question. Some of these categories no longer work, others have never worked, and others need to be corrected. We must acknowledge that there has been no counter-subjectivity formed within this process that is capable of overturning it—or if there has been, it has been formed only in a limited sense. The exhaustion of those theoretical attempts that, from the end of the 1980s onward, made reference to operaismo was a result of their incapacity to rethink or go beyond these categories, and so rethink and go beyond themselves. They transformed operaismo into something it had never been, namely, a school of thought, useful only for gaining academic positions at universities; or even a church, with its grotesque lineup of popes, liturgies, and sacred scriptures—perhaps a heretical orthodoxy, with its own niche in the market alongside other traditional Marxist orthodoxies. But operaismo, as we have seen, was never a heresy: for operaismo Marx and Lenin were not sacred scriptures to be restored but powerful tools to be transformed and used. Again, a Machiavellian return to first principles is called for. As Tronti writes: "The historic parties of the workers' movement have had an easy time because to their left there have always been (and still are)

Zarathustra-type blowhards who go around promising to tear down the world but wouldn't be able to tell you how to brush the dust off their ancient sacred texts."[13]

We can find traces of this in the collapse of UniNomade, a website that between 2010 and 2013 tried to rethink the political role of journals, with mixed results.[14] Within the group different positions emerged, came into conflict, and ultimately separated. The split largely centered around two issues: the relationship with the Left and the relationship between theory and practice. Negri and those around him claimed that the crisis of the Left opened up space for the real dangers of fascism, and thus the Left needed to be rebuilt. They also held that an autonomy of the concept was necessary with respect to political practice, bringing an end to coresearch and the concept of class composition. Put simply: the intellectuals broke with the militants to create a think tank that claimed to supply the discourse for a renewed left political representation. The overturning was complete and canceled out the origin: the "post-" eats up operaismo, the intellectual renounces the militant, the autonomy of politics becomes the autonomy of philosophy. Tragedy is repeated as farce, farce as cabaret. The "post-" returns to the "pre-" and to that sacred family of which operaismo was never a part: the Left.

Here we find examples of personal issues and individual opportunism that speak volumes about the subjectivities involved. The reasons we want to explore these are not moral but entirely political: taking up Guido Borio's analysis in the previous chapter, we want to analyze the material relationships at work in the production of subjectivity. When there were strong political movements there was a sort of virtuous triangle created between the different levels: on the top, those given autonomy of thought who broke with their own systemic location; at the base, those organizing struggles who needed concepts that could be used as tools to force the present, a theoretical arsenal able to guide the way; in the middle, those able to translate the discourse to the bottom and correct the line toward the top. In the absence of political movements, this triangle was fragmented, and each part went off on its own. The militants located at the bottom were drawn into daily struggles without any room to breathe strategically; the intellectuals located at the top narcissistically reflected themselves in their own concepts. As Alquati taught us, to create their space in the market the intellectuals needed to project onto concretely mythicized social subjects "a series of historical categories in which they collect all the ideological repression of the isolation forced upon them by the system or by the guilt that they feel at a certain point for their capitulation to the bosses of the culture industry."[15] Although written sixty years ago, these words still speak to us today (you need only think of how many careers have been built on the ideological projection of migrant struggles, and how these same thinkers often dissociate themselves from the complexities of concrete struggles and of flesh and blood migrants when they actually call into question the forms of life and privileges of the functionaries of the culture industry).

Looking back we can see there were subjective limits with respect to organization. As Alquati already showed in his 1961 text quoted above, intellectual hubris leads to an ignoring of the process of the formation of a militant and social counter-subjectivity, instead imagining that there is immediacy, necessity, and spontaneity between the identification of supposed tendencies and their realization. In this way organization as a process disappears, leaving only the dead end of conceptual abstraction. Remember the definitions given by Guido Borio: Tronti is characterized by his attention to the *political*, Negri to the *subject*, Alquati to the *process*. We could say that at the moment in which the subject and the political stopped recomposing themselves within the process, to the extent to which these two elements became autonomous, separating from each other and therefore cutting themselves off from the third, the problem of revolutionary organization became a black hole for operaismo. The autonomy of political administration and the autonomy of political philosophy were the result of this separation.

Thus, if in the history we have sketched above we see people born within a political environment getting sucked into the culture industry, now we have people born within the culture industry who use the political environment for their own ends, described here by Tronti:

> One of the greatest riches of this experience (something that I want to emphasize) was the exceptional personalities that were involved in it. The best moments of *Quaderni rossi* and of *Classe operaia* were the meetings organized to write and prepare the journal and the newspaper. I always say, also to younger people, that I have never found that type of person again, I have never found them again. Later I was back in the party, not to speak of other even worse places that came after, like the university, the intellectuals. That [former] type of person was a truly miraculous emergence in their great human richness, their lack of ambition, things that today seem inconceivable. But with regard to all those I met afterward, they were always people whose central interest was their own personal ambition, to find themselves a place here, to find themselves a place there, both in the party and in culture. There wasn't a trace of this in that [earlier] period.[16]

So, after the time of giants, the time arrived not only of dwarves but of fawning courtiers. And it is for these figures that operaismo becomes an icon or a brand to be sectioned off, with which to earn their incomes or build their careers. These are the followers of operaismo as a school of thought, who jostle to climb onto the stage of so-called Italian Theory or to get recognized in the media. Once again, this isn't a question of moral judgment; it is a political problem. We are not talking about the tired call to get your hands dirty. The point is that an intellectual moved by antagonism, who wants to break with themselves and become a militant, shouldn't be scared of getting their ideas dirty.

The main problem we are left with is the crisis of what is in the middle. This is what Alquati calls the intermediary militant, or rather the militant that is rooted on the medium range. Without this figure there is a separateness between the top—that closes itself up in intellectual self-referentiality—and the base—that basks in the self-referentiality of practice. But note that when we speak of high and base levels we are not talking about hierarchies of importance: on the contrary, the barycenter is located in the middle, in the strategic possibility of acting as a hinge between the different levels, to constantly transform that which is below and that which is above, to construct a project through a spiral process able to break down the separateness imposed by the enemy and to recompose the fragmented forces into a macro-collective that is subjectively rich and organizationally powerful.

The intermediary is the most important and most uncomfortable role: in most periods you are on your own. It doesn't allow you to shelter in the recognition of a community, either that of the day-to-day militant or that of intellectual abstraction, both of which are products of defeatism and an acceptance of the status quo. It is the location of those who don't limit themselves to taking note of things as they happen, but continually attempt to anticipate them, those who problematize and call into question what there already is, who attempt to grasp what it could become, who destroy their individual ambition to construct collective ends. The intermediary is therefore the strategic, fundamental, decisive militant—when there are struggles, and even more so when there are none.

In conclusion we return to the initial question of this chapter: What is left of operaismo? We will now retrace the response that we've outlined in the previous pages. We do this in a context that is in some ways a reversal of the 1960s from the point of view of the relations of force and of the relationship between class composition and crisis. The struggles of the mass worker were actually anti-cyclical struggles; they happened within and against the expansion of capitalist development, in its so-called economic boom. In that phase growing expectations were created, which the struggles at the time used against capitalist accumulation and work, producing a crisis of the wage regime, or rather its inflation (if the boss offers us ten, we want 100, if they offer us 100, we want 1,000). Today we are faced with the opposite scenario: the crisis of the recession has created a climate of decreasing expectations, so if the boss is wary about offering ten, we are happy with five or even with nothing.[17]

One problem that still remains unresolved is that of new conflictual subjects. As we have seen, those who have tried to simply extract these subjects from the technical composition have failed. Again, we need to overturn our point of view, and to do so we must return to first principles. In the full consciousness that the history of operaismo is over, we must begin from the method. As the operaisti reread Marx and Lenin against Marxism-Leninism, we must reread operaismo against the "post-": its "post-" and all the "posts." Tronti puts it well in *Con le spalle al futuro* (With our backs to the future): "The post is a legacy of events: it is given to you as a surplus. The *beyond* is a product of the will: you must deserve it to have it."[18]

(We have spiraled back again to the question of temporality. Insofar as "new-ism" forces us into innovation's increasingly short time span, it is capital's terrain—it impedes the possibility of counter-subjectivation, continuously impoverishing and fragmenting our abilities. Thus the problem is how to appropriate an autonomous temporality in a break with the temporality of capital, how to ensure the long-term accumulation of counter-subjectivity where capital imposes destructive consumption, how to accelerate rupture where capital imposes long-term accumulation.)

Summarizing their main points below, we will see what the operaist method and style consist in, and that together they make up the *point of view*. We do not claim here to capture all of the complexity of the point of view, but to simplify it in order to render it politically useful.

The partial point of view of an autonomous side that is to be built. This is the side not of the exploited but of those who struggle against exploitation. Not of those who work for a living, but of those who struggle against work in order to live freely. Not of the poor and the victims, perverse objects of priestly and missionary desires, but of the working class (that, we will never tire of repeating, is a question of the qualitative power of recomposition and not of calloused hands and dirty blue overalls). The question is whether it is possible for there to be a new workers' subjectivity (*operaietà*) that is a central force. This is what we should be looking for, in a continual search for a central contradiction, not to resolve it but to take it to its extreme consequences. As Tronti writes: "From the working-class point of view, capital's contradictions should neither be rejected nor resolved but only utilised. But making use of these contradictions also demands that we exacerbate them."[19]

The point of view of conflict. Our collective side is something to be built; it is not handed to us objectively by capital. It is to be constructed in struggle: there is no class without class struggle. So operaismo searches for the friend-enemy opposition as a form of political and militant action. As Tronti put it recently, in *Dello spirito libero* (Of the free spirit): "Political friendship is that which those who are against have in common, that which brings them together. And the action of being against consecrates great friendships."[20] That which deepens the enemy's contradictions is good; that which resolves them is bad. It is by starting from the *against* that we construct our *for*.

The point of view of subjectivity, or rather of *counter-subjectivity*. This hasn't got anything to do with the current use of the term "subjectivity." In recent decades (in the time of the "post-") there has been a very weak interpretation of subjectivity, mostly linked to Foucauldianism and the umpteenth "post-": post-structuralism (for which Foucault and the post-structuralists are partly but not entirely responsible). The discovery of subjectivity was understood as the discovery of something "good" that put aside the question of class, the collective side, the subject in the recomposed sense. It was the rediscovery of the centrality of the individual, and so a capitulation to the order of liberal discourse, whether in its paleo or neo form. Neither is the subjectivity we're talking about attributable to consciousness and what, as we have seen, it meant to the Marxist tradition—the element of idealistic mediation in historical progress.

The subjectivity that is at the center of operaismo and the definition of class composition is radically different from and contrary to these weak interpretations. Subjectivity isn't good: it is a battlefield. The production of subjectivity in capitalism is intrinsic to the social relation of production and exploitation; it is the stakes of an antagonistic process of *formazione*, that is, of conflict, violence, reproduction, consensus, and transformation.

When, in today's context, in which the relations of force favor capital, we speak of "proletarian subjectivity" (or of the precarious or of living labor or whatever way you wish to identify the potential collectivity on our side), we are speaking of a subjectivity forged above all by capitalist domination. Counter-subjectivity means a subjectivity that isn't only against capital but also against the capital within us. Because, to the extent to which we hate the bosses, we must start to hate ourselves and that cancer that devours us daily and puts us at the service of those who exploit us. Worse still, it renders us satisfied with this situation, makes us feel recognized and grateful. Thus, the first problem that we find ourselves facing in phases like this is a rupture with the acceptance of a subjectivity shaped by the enemy. That is, the ability not to accept the existent, the time that is consigned to us: the capacity to be untimely, to be within and against our time. Materialists, realists, and, untimely: a materialism of untimeliness. As long as history is occupied by the enemy, we need to spray it with bullets, without crying over the present.

The point of view of the tendency. Tendency doesn't mean the objectivity and linearity of the path of History; it isn't a synonym of teleology; it doesn't have anything to do with predicting the future. And, obviously, tendency doesn't mean the irreversibility of the process, which is the dogma at the basis of the innovationist and accelerationist religion. On the contrary, as these processes are founded on and molded by relations of force, they can be continually interrupted, deviated, and overturned. The concept of tendency describes the capacity to see the possibility of a development of opposition and radical alterity in the composition of the elements that make up the present. Tendency is like prophecy: it means seeing and expressing in a different and antagonistic way that which already exists virtually in the present.

Once again, the lesson of operaismo, and of the line in it that can be defined as *compositionist*—which makes class composition into a method of militant action—is the need to grasp the terrain of conflictual possibility within the ambivalences and ambiguities of already existing subjectivity and behaviors. Tendency means anticipation, a political wager. Without a political wager there is no politics in a revolutionary sense, but only the administration of the existent, or rather the technique of institutional politics. The most important period for revolutionary militants is when there aren't any struggles. If they arrive when struggles are already happening, they are too late.

The point of view of recomposition. The tendency is therefore a question of the composition of the various elements. Political composition always implies a double process: recomposition for our own autonomous ends and the decomposition of the ends of the enemy. Recomposition isn't a sum of the elements as they are, but their transformation into a process of rupture with the current context, and the construction of a new one. Thus, we aren't talking about reunifying a supposed original unity fragmented by the actions of capitalism, returning to what was there before. Class recomposition is, rather, the collective creation of an autonomous subject. We could say that recomposition is the return to a possible autonomy that doesn't exist. A return to the elements that, breaking with the given context, are composed in a radically different way, creating a new context of social relations. And through recomposing themselves in the rupture, these elements subvert themselves and change their essence; their original function is overturned.

We also know that capital continuously decomposes, composes, and recomposes, that it destroys and transforms, in what is called innovation. Innovation is always capitalist: it responds not to mere productive needs but to our enemy's necessity to defeat a determinate political composition. We can therefore say that the *opposite of innovation isn't conservation, but revolution.* If for innovation and conservation we substitute the terms "left" and "right" the answer is the same: *the opposite of right isn't left, but revolution.* For this reason, we can't define ourselves as left-wing: not because the Left has become a certain way, but because it has always been that way. From its Enlightenment origins, the Left has been progressivist and innovationist. It is the thought of victimhood and of defeat, of compatibility with the power of capital and of the excommunication of antagonistic power, of trust in History and of hostility toward those who struggle against their own time.

In light of this, operaismo is *the point of view of those who are free, the point of view of autonomy*. This is the essence of the operaist overturning: first the class, then capital. This is not a hypothesis that we must put to universal empirical verification, even if it is often empirically verified. It is the affirmation of a rupture, of a rupture with subordinate thought and with a dependence on History.

It is difficult these days to talk of freedom; it is a word tarnished not only by neoliberalism or by the right, but most of all by democracy. Freedom in the service of exploitation, the freedom of tolerance and of the politically correct, the freedom to say and do what you want as long as everything that you say and do is irrelevant to the relationships of domination. It is the freedom of the individual to accept the domination of capital, separating themselves from a possible collective process of opposition and alterity, of the construction of autonomy. That kind of freedom is not a right to claim, but an enemy to fight. A radical critique of democracy is an urgent task, because democracy is entirely in the enemy camp. Democracy is an infernal machine of depoliticization: it is the true anti-politics, or rather the political form of anti-politics.

As a hypothesis of theoretical and practical militant research, let's suggest that *the opposite of democracy isn't oppression, but freedom*. To those who today repeat that we must retreat to Frontist positions because there is a fascist danger, we respond that the main danger is that which is already fully deployed, which is democracy. We must not retreat even further, but begin to advance, for an anti-liberal freedom, an autonomous freedom, a communist freedom, an operaist freedom. A freedom that is simultaneously an exercise in counter-power and the practice of a collective force. The freedom of those who declare: You can't catch us!

This leads us to the *point of view of elusiveness*. We can't content ourselves with anticipating lines of tendency if we then don't have the capacity and the force to take them up as weapons against the history of capital. At the same time, we can't wallow in theoretical and practical victories, because if we aren't able to leap forward again those victories will immediately be subsumed by our enemy, becoming innovations and not ruptures. Anticipation, problematization, and reorientation, then a new anticipation: this is the method that Alquati taught us in his practice. When you thought you had understood something and repeated it to him, he would question it and force you to take another leap forward. Because only by continually leaping forward, at the cost of living in apparent solitude, can we truly become elusive. But this is never an individual solitude, because it is always a militant search for a collective tendency. It is not the solitude of the intellectual, who is truly alone even when they seem to be in the company of many others like them or under them. It is the apparent solitude of an avant-garde rooted in a line of material force, that won't accept the misery of the already given but ceaselessly searches for the fullness of the possible.

If the context in many ways has been overturned with respect to the '60s, it has traits in common with the 1950s, which we described as the "breeding ground" of operaismo. But only *ex post* can we describe the 1950s in this way, only *ex post* can we think of what happened as if it was necessary, or at least easily predictable. It wasn't. And the same is true today. "Nothing is happening," the Left repeats incessantly. While the radical Left yells, "Let's resist, defend ourselves and reproduce ourselves!," getting carried away in the lexicon of rights and of humanitarian reason, ranting with the contemptible sadness of senile wisdom or with the thinly disguised opportunism of individual fear. We respond with the strength of the operaist method:

What will never function is the cold logic of reason when it is not moved by class hatred. We should concede nothing—other than a healthy dose of disdain—to the philistine who reproaches Marx for having constantly seen the revolution behind the corner and

Lenin for having wanted it in the improper time and moment. An elementary rule of practical conduct ought to be immediately—intuitively—applied in these cases. When, on the one hand, we find those who say that tomorrow everything will blow up and the old world will crumble, and, on the other hand, we find those who say that nothing is going to budge for fifty years, and the former are denied by the facts and the second proven correct, we are with the former—here, we must be with those who are mistaken.[21]

Appendix: Beyond Operaismo and So-Called Post-Operaismo

Davide Gallo Lassere: Operaismo, the Italian political workerism of the 1960s, was among other things characterized by its rediscovery of Marx against Marxism. Can you explain what that means?[1]

Gigi Roggero: Operaismo is a Machiavellian return to principles: it is a return to Marx against Marxism, against its tradition of determinism, historicism, and objectivism. Operaismo isn't a heresy within the Marxist family; it is a rupture with that family. The operaisti defined themselves as Marxian and not Marxist, a bit like the elderly Marx, who declared, "Je ne suis pas marxiste." However, this return to principles wasn't aimed at building a new orthodoxy based on a correct reading of the word of the prophet, as had been attempted by the various heresies (such as the Trotskyists and the Bordigists, who, ennobled by Stalinist persecution, had often paradoxically ended up attacking Stalin as deviating from the line of a linear historical development traced once and for all by Marx). The operaist reading of Marx wasn't only against Marxism, but in a certain sense was critical of the limits and the blind alleys in Marx himself, stretching and forcing his words to make their ambivalences explode, looking for weapons with which to attack the factory-society of contemporary capitalism.

Unlike previous workerisms (such as councilism) or contemporary ones (such as those of a Christian or populist kind), Italian operaismo didn't glorify workers and proletarians: it wagered on the possibility that there was a force in them that they could mobilize against themselves, not to extend but to destroy their own condition. It was therefore a workerism against work, refusing a naturalized subjectivity imposed by the capital relation. It was a workerism based on the irreducible partiality of the point of view, on an autonomous partisan autonomy that needed to be built.

In their rupture with universalism, with Marxism, and partly with Marx, the operaisti made the question of subjectivity central, or rather—as Alquati called it—of counter-subjectivity. This was a subjectivity that wasn't only against capital, but also against the capital within us.

The operaist inversion must be understood in light of the irreducible partiality of the point of view: first the class, then capital. Capital is not the subject of History, it is not that which does and undoes, that which determines development and the conditions for its own overcoming. Rather, history is non-teleological, and at its center is class struggle, its power of refusal and its autonomy.

DGL: Mario Tronti undoubtedly made a significant contribution on this point . . .

GR: With Tronti class stopped being a merely sociological and descriptive concept, becoming an entirely political concept. Class doesn't exist naturally, or rather it exists in the nature of capital as a taxonomy of the social segments available within the labor market. There can be proletarians without a proletariat, workers without a working class. Class is a question not of stratification but of counterposition. It is struggle that produces class as a partisan collectivity: class means class antagonism. As Tronti says: there is no class without class struggle.

This is one of the issues that requires both a use and a stretching of Marx: we should use his historical works, which show the proletarians became a class on the 1848 barricades; and should stretch the (ambivalent) Marx of *Capital*, whose first volume shows that it was struggles and not bourgeois legislation or enlightened capitalists that determined the reduction of the working day. It is interesting to note that C. L. R. James came to the same conclusions as the operaisti in the same period, in his 1966–1967 lectures, now collected in the book, *You Don't Play with Revolution*: if the bosses could make us work all day without resistance or conflict, they would. This must be remembered by those who complain today about free work, who call for the redistribution of wealth as a moral principle, and who think that a "citizens' income" is a question of productive rationality. Only struggle can force the bosses to pay up; the wage represents the spoils of war. With all due respect to the Left, if one side doesn't fight, the other will take no prisoners.

We can also use the third volume of *Capital*, which is famously cut short at the unfinished chapter on class. In *Workers and Capital*, Tronti ironically notes that "every now and then someone, from Renner to Dahrendorf, has a grand old time of completing what had remained incomplete, and what results from all this is libel against Marx, which should, at a minimum, be punished with physical violence."[2] Already in Chapter 50 of *Capital*, vol. 3, "Illusions Created by Competition," Marx writes that it isn't competition that regulates the price of labor but the price of labor that regulates competition. By arguing that it was struggles that determined capital—first the class, then capital—the Italian operaisti showed that interpreting capital starting from the point of view of capital was an ideological projection. When people today say, "It's what the markets want," they remain within this projection. In the unfinished chapter on class, Marx makes only a few points, but they are nevertheless quite important. He says that it is not just income that creates a class, or simply your location within production relations, much as these obviously determine the material base upon which the question of class is founded: class is created by struggle that breaks with the abstract democratic unity of the people. It is created when the "'indivisible' people" break into "enemy camps."[3] As Tronti writes, "when *the working class* refuses politically to become *the people*, it in fact opens up the most direct path to the socialist revolution."[4] One is divided into two: the non-recomposable for capital becomes the possibility of recomposition for the class. The class disappears as a merely social aggregate and becomes an antagonistic subject irreducible to the unity of the general interest, which is the interest of capital. It is this assumption of workers' partiality that forces the capitalists to aggregate politically, to overcome their own contradictions, to discover themselves as a social power, collectively using the power of their enemy to develop and leap forward. Any illusions of a peaceful evolution disappear for reformists on both sides. The mask of democracy falls to reveal the true face of the relation of force between the two conflicting powers: no longer labor and capital, but laborers and capitalists, class against class, force against force.

Operaismo is a thought of refusal and a thought of the negative as the foundation of communism. What deepens the contradictions of the enemy is good, what resolves them is bad. The contradiction isn't resolvable within the organic composition of capital, that is, in the relationship between variable capital and constant capital, but must be made to explode in a conflict between the organic composition of capital and class composition, or rather, in the relationship between the articulation of labor power and the production of subjectivity. The operaist reading of Marx starts from this and then heads off in a direction that is distinct from and opposed to Marxism.

DGL: You referred to class composition. Can you clarify how operaismo worked politically with the class composition of Italy at the time through the practice of workers' inquiry?

GR: In recent years workers' inquiry and coresearch have been much talked about, perhaps even too much, in the sense that it would be better to talk about them less and practice them more. Often comrades think of inquiry as a specialism, a rhetoric, or a confirmation of the things that we already do (given we're precarious, if we do a self-inquiry our point of view will be the point of view of the precariat!). Nothing could be more pointless. Coresearch is actually an autonomous political process taking place together with the production of counter-knowledge, counter-subjectivity, and counter-organization, in which the counter-use of the capitalist means of production (including specific skills) also leads to their transformation. The militant is always looking for something that they don't yet understand, a possible force to make the contradictions explode, something that already exists but that they can't yet see. Militants are either restless or they are not militants.

In the 1950s and at the beginning of the 1960s, when Alquati and his comrades began carrying out coresearch, the workers and the factories had been politically abandoned. In a sort of unconscious Frankfurtism, the Italian Communist Party (PCI) held that the working class was now irreversibly integrated into the capitalist machine. In this way, a vicious circle was created. The PCI—which had chosen to follow the middle classes and the "Italian road to socialism" (a road without revolutionary class struggle)—asked the factory militants if anything was stirring, and they confirmed the line at the top, saying that there was no possibility of revolutionary class struggle among the workers. Immigrants from Southern Italy who had been inserted into the production line, who a few years later would become the "mass worker," were seen by the PCI and trade union militants at the time as passive and alienated opportunists. However, the operaist militants, when talking with these young "new forces," revealed real ambivalence in their behavior: it was true that they often voted for the reactionary trade unions, but that was because they didn't feel represented by anyone; they didn't take part in the strikes because they thought they were useless. The operaisti showed that even their passivity was potentially more effective as a form of struggle. And very soon their outsider status at work turned into refusal and insubordination. What's more, these Southern Italians who had immigrated into the industrial metropoles of Northern Italy bore little resemblance to their representation in left-wing literature and cinema, of victims laden down with cardboard boxes, needing our tears and sympathy. On the contrary, they were a potential force, bringing with them new behaviors and cultures of conflict foreign to the traditions of the workers' movement institutions, which now co-managed exploitation in the factory. Enough with the tears, with talking about the needs of the victim, with the culture of the Left: the revolutionary militant searches for strength, not weakness. That's why we say operaismo is a communist experience that breaks with the Communist Party and which is foreign to the culture of the Left.

But this search for force is never based on ideology or on the satisfaction of its own identity. It is always a political wager rooted within a historically determined class composition.

DGL: Dealing with class composition means posing the subjective problem of political recomposition. What is meant by recomposition? Is it more about synthesis or rupture?

GR: Adding to what I said earlier, we could now say that there is no class struggle without class recomposition. First, though, we have to know what we mean by class composition, and to understand the relationship between technical composition and political composition, that is, between the capitalist articulation of labor power in its relationship with machines and the formation of the class as an independent subject. Technical composition and political composition don't provide us with a static picture of the different elements, of labor power as totally subordinate to capital on one side and the class as totally autonomous on the other. They are both processes that are crossed with conflict and with the possibility of rupture and overturning, because both operate within the social relation of capital as an antagonistic relation. There is no conciliatory dialectic between these two processes, just as there is no synthesis and symmetry. The central or most advanced subject for capitalist accumulation isn't necessarily the central and most advanced subject for struggle, as was thought in the social communist tradition, and as was often implicitly taken up in analyses of so-called post-Fordism. There is no re-proposing of the Marxist relationship between class in itself and class for itself, mediated by an idealistic class consciousness that must simply be revealed. As we have already said many times, subjectivity—the base and the stakes of class composition—is not consciousness. Subjectivity isn't revealed, it is produced. Capital produces it, and so can struggles.

Political composition always implies a double process: recomposition for our own autonomous ends and the decomposition of the ends of the enemy. Recomposition isn't a summary of things as they are, but their transformation into a process of rupture with the current situation toward the construction of a new one. Recomposing themselves in the rupture, the different elements are subverted, their essence is changed, their original function overturned.

Capital also continuously decomposes, composes, and recomposes; that is, it constantly destroys and transforms, in what it calls innovation. Capital primarily responded to the revolutionary movements of the 1960s and '70s not with repression but with innovation. Innovation is an inverse revolution aiming toward a profound change in what Alquati called the medium and base levels of reality,[5] able to reinforce the reproduction of the high levels, that is, the accumulation of domination and capital. This change bears the marks of conflict with its enemy, the proletariat, which has now been deprived of the possibility of rupture, subsumed and turned toward systemic ends. For example, capital responded to the struggles against salaried work and workers' and proletarians' flexible autonomy with increased precariousness. Starting from the 1980s and 1990s, in the height of neoliberal development, there was, on the one hand, those who called for the return to the shackles of a permanent job, forgetting that these shackles were something that workers and proletarians had previously refused and fought against, and that the new situation bore the marks of this conflict; and, on the other hand, those who mistook innovation for revolution, fantasizing that social cooperation had become fully free and autonomous, leaving capital as nothing but a parasitic shell. Neither saw the continuity of and the possibility for antagonism, and thus both assumed the separation between the two classes had already happened: for the former this meant the impossibility of liberation, for the latter that liberation had already taken place. Both are ideological positions, both are impotent, forgetting the problem of revolutionary rupture. And neither see the central issue of class composition as a process that is continuously crossed with conflict.

DGL: On this subject, Romano Alquati—who was very important within operaismo, although underrated in Italy and almost unknown outside the country—talked about "organized spontaneity." What did he mean?

GR: The configurations of class composition and recomposition that I have outlined here mainly come from Alquati. To put it briefly, there is no operaismo without Alquati, although Alquati cannot be reduced solely to the operaist experience. Often he's seen as the "inventor of coresearch," an identity he refused by saying that militants had always done coresearch: he did coresearch because he was a militant. He argued that it was like saying that if I put on shoes to cross a street full of stones it meant I had invented shoes. There was obviously a paradoxical exaggeration in this, because coresearch as we mean it today, or which we are attempting to reinvent, is founded above all on Alquati's contribution and on the collectives built by him to put it into practice. However, it is true that defining him simply as the inventor of coresearch limits his contribution to the 1960s and his important writings on FIAT and Olivetti. Alquati is more than that. His research within and against the "middle-class university" in the 1970s was fundamental, foreseeing the emergence of the social worker and the intellectual proletariat. Between the 1980s and 1990s he developed a complex model of the functioning of capitalism that he called the *modellone*, aimed at the revolutionary macro-objective of rupture and liberation from capitalist civilization. In that period Alquati showed extraordinary foresight on themes, issues, and questions (from hyper-industrialization to the centrality of the reproduction of human capacity) that today have proved to be decisive.

His definition of "organized spontaneity" emerges from coresearch undertaken in the flesh and blood of the workers' struggles of the 1960s. The workers' movement traditions understood there to be a division between the cult of spontaneity and the fetish of organization, seeing them as operating within a dialectic following stages of development: first there is spontaneity, then there is organization. Alquati definitively broke with this dialectic and proposed an apparent oxymoron: at FIAT there was no external organization that produced conflict, but neither was it simply spontaneity that created it. A sort of "invisible organization" had been created through which the workers communicated, prepared struggles, scheduled their attacks, and blocked the factory. It was this invisible organization that posed itself as the avant-garde of the recompositional process, while the party militants were left behind, following hesitantly and in fact often acting as an obstacle.

Going beyond the specificity of those struggles, the question of organized spontaneity allows us to correctly locate this relationship in political terms, to distinguish spontaneity from spontaneism—which makes it into an ideology—and organization from mere management. The two terms of the relationship are never separated and opposed: spontaneity has to feed organization and organization must take place within spontaneity. We could say that workers' autonomy is organization that reflects on its own spontaneity, and spontaneity that reflects on its own organization. And the party (in a way that is radically different from its current use and meaning) is the subject that continually recomposes the relationship between spontaneity and organization, between negation and macro-ends—which are precisely the issues that remained unresolved in the operaist experience and in that which followed it.

DGL: In your writings you often refer to the "method of the tendency": What is that exactly?

GR: This method is central and, perhaps more than most, often misunderstood. Some figures stemming from operaismo interpreted the tendency in increasingly mechanistic terms, as if the lines of capitalist development directly handed us subjects capable of social transformation. So instead of being a rupture with technical composition, political composition became its product. This mechanism, which was a simple ideological inversion, was identified as an ontology: the subjects produced by capitalist development were considered to be ontologically revolutionary subjects. And so, in order for their analysis to work, they had to forget the issues of class composition, of relations of force, of the processes of struggle through which subjectivity forms and breaks with the process of capitalist subjectivation.

From the revolutionary point of view, tendency doesn't mean the objectivity and linearity of the path of History and doesn't have anything to do with foreseeing the future. It's best to leave meteorologists to predict the rain. As militants we must create storms. And obviously tendency doesn't mean the irreversibility of the process, which is the dogma at the base of the innovationist and accelerationist religions. On the contrary, as it is founded on and molded by relations of force, the process can be continually interrupted, deviated, and overturned. Tendency thus means the capacity to grasp the possibilities for an oppositional and radically diverse development within the composition of the present. Tendency is like prophecy: it means seeing and affirming in a different way something that already exists virtually.

In brief, tendency means anticipation. It is the capacity of grasping the terrain of antagonistic possibility within the ambivalences and ambiguities of the existing composition, subjectivity, and behavior. Tendency means a political wager. The wager is not about throwing dice, nor about making a scientific forecast, but about choosing a path. It is about identifying a line that doesn't exist but could. It is a materialist wager, within and against the existing relations of force. Without a political wager there is no politics in a revolutionary sense, but only the administration of what exists, or rather the techniques of institutional politics.

In the mid-1970s, writing on the issues of *formazione* and the university, Alquati said that coresearch was needed so as not to simply be following on the tail of the movement: "Research [is] aimed at foreseeing and anticipating, not at ideologically rationalizing what has already happened gradually, which 'spontaneously' happens when the mass 'moves.' The problem is general: finding a strategy needed to guide us, and a political direction that is able to anticipate according to a strategy. There is no point turning up too late."[6] The militant must take the risk. The important thing is to act within and against the materiality of the existent, and not—as often happened in what is called "post-operaismo"—within one's own individual fantasy and against collective possibilities.

DGL: To the two best-known names on an international level—Mario Tronti and Toni Negri—can be ascribed two varieties of operaismo that you refer to as "katechontic" and "accelerationist." Through figures like Romano Alquati or Sergio Bologna, however, it is possible to identify a third theoretical and political paradigm within operaismo, which we could define as "compositionist." Why is it important to deepen that line of research?

GR: It is through this paradigm (defined here as compositionist, though you could easily use another term) and its introduction of the decisive element of subjectivity that operaismo was able to break the partially closed system of Marxian logic, which risks remaining trapped in explanations of how to produce and reproduce the iron cage. Subjectivity isn't formed deterministically from material location; neither is it formed separately from it: as we have already seen, subjectivity is linked to struggle, that is, to the potential capital has to shape it and to the possibility of behaviors and forces that are formed against capital. Using coresearch and acting within class composition to bend it in an antagonistic direction means continually centering political initiative on the relationship between process and subject. Put simply: in a process in which the relations of force favor capital, the subject will be primarily shaped by it; in a process with different relations of force, a different subject will be formed. To say that the subject is shaped by capital, as happens at present, doesn't at all mean there are no possibilities for conflict and autonomy. Alquati talked about an "unresolved residue," unresolvable, that is, for capital, which he attributed to the active human capacity on which capital must continuously feed to make its system work. We could even say that there is a potential structural asymmetry between the two classes: while capital needs the proletariat, the proletariat doesn't need capital, and in the end neither does it need itself as a product of that social relationship. This is the irresolvable contradiction for capital from which the permanent possibility of antagonism derives, which assumes forms that are expressed differently at different times, and in some periods remain implicit.

Antagonism can't be messianically awaited, nor imagined by beginning from what we want—like the theorists of the multitude did, who, when the proletarians didn't behave in the way they would have liked them to, intellectually ran ahead on their own, deciding, to paraphrase Brecht, that if the multitude doesn't agree, then we should appoint a new one. But militants must dig in the ambivalences and the ambiguities (with concepts even before using their hands), in the "dirt" of real behaviors: not to glorify them in a populist manner but to search for a politics in them at the level of their intrinsic forms and expression, to find something virtual that has not yet been transformed into a collective act. For example, before becoming an explicit and collective form of opposition and negation, the refusal of work was incarnated in fragmented refusals on an individual level. There isn't a necessary path through developmental stages from an intrinsic politics to an explicit politics. Instead, the path must be built through processes of organization, coresearch, the power of the militant wager. We could say that the search for an intrinsic politics is the search for a space between the abstract potentiality of antagonism and its overt expression; it is the space in which behaviors can take different or even opposing directions; it is the space in which the process can be concretely deviated, steered, interrupted, and overturned. It is the space of militant intervention.

The problem, then, is that both the "accelerationist" and the "katechontic" paradigms (the katechon is, in Pauline theology, the force that holds back evil) end up assuming the temporality of capitalist development and deriving from it both class composition and its revolutionary possibilities. In the first paradigm we simply need to accelerate the development of the new technical composition to transform it into a political composition; in the second we need to retain the force of the old political composition to fight the technical composition. Both risk considering development at a level of abstraction that loses contact with the medium range, the level at which there is a concrete possibility of rupture and overthrowal. Yet the method of the tendency that interests us is not about identifying an "objective" development but about posing the problem of interruption and deviation, that is, of the accumulation of force to construct recompositional processes. This force is accumulated as much in acceleration as in holding back, and its strength in one or the other depends on the period and above all on the struggles that determine resistance and that propel us forward. Thus, it is from the point of view of class composition, its potential autonomy and its possibility for revolutionary transformation, that we must evaluate the possibilities of acceleration or of holding back.

But in Negri's accelerationism, tendency becomes teleology. The process of organization, conflict, and rupture that takes place within the relationships between technical composition, political composition, and recomposition is substituted with an immediatism—an immediate translation of technical composition into political composition. He ends up ignoring the process and immediately identifying the subject as ontologically free and autonomous. He doesn't realize that the subject is not in fact free and autonomous, but profoundly marked by capitalist subjectivation. Only by grasping the ambivalences and bending them in an antagonistic direction can we be opposed to ourselves as capitalist subjects. Only through the process of struggle can the subject win their liberty and autonomy. Negri has the intellectual vice of not measuring his categories according to militancy within and against reality, but measuring reality according to his categories. The autonomy of political philosophy follows the autonomy of the political. Nonexistent victories are proclaimed, hiding what is actually resignation to defeat. It's sadly paradoxical that someone who had talked about the hegemony of the "general intellect" ends his journey in the conceited solitude of the individual intellect.

DGL: Operaismo has often been accused of being developmentalist...

GR: In some ways that's justified, mainly in its evolution as "post-operaismo," in which tendency became teleology. However, the rhetoric against development that has become so widespread in recent decades is equally problematic, or maybe even more so, because it often ends up assuming moralistic and class traits, by which I mean traits of the other class. It is quite easy to support degrowth while sipping on a cognac in your comfy office in the Sorbonne... Not all positions against development are reducible to degrowth, but even the best of them, those most interested in struggles, risk mirroring their polemical object. In fact, in both developmentalism and anti-developmentalism the real point is lost and they both become rather ideological: one imagines the revolutionary subject in everything that is produced by the development of capital; the other imagines it in everything that precedes capital or that is illusorily regarded as being "outside" that development. One option is so much inside that it forgets to be against, and so ends up getting sucked into the jaws of an impossible reformism; the other invokes a powerful attack from the outside, trusting itself to an unrealistic spontaneism. Materialism without revolutionary will slips into determinism; revolutionary will deprived of materialism slips into idealism. Whether we like it or not, we are inside development and its chaotic contradictions, and so we must analyze it in a similarly ambivalent and conflictual manner. We must understand how much counter-subjectivity and antagonistic possibility are created and destroyed within development, how much they are created and destroyed in resistance or in the act of propelling the process forward. The counter-use of the process means not only using tools produced by development for other ends, but doing this by bending them, transforming them, and creating new tools. As being within isn't a question of individual desires or existential experience but is simply the hard materiality of the social relationship that we are fighting, the point is how to be against.

The dialectic between developmentalism and anti-developmentalism, acceleration and degrowth, modernity and anti-modernity, is thus situated within the point of view of capital. Capital is composed through a variable combination of acceleration and holding back; it destroys the composition of its own antagonist and recomposes the fragments that are produced according to its developmental needs. So the problem for the militant is how to think development from the point of view of our real or potential side, to retain the elements that impede the destructive acceleration of the capitalist innovation that impoverishes us, and to accelerate the elements that produce a rupture in the enemy, enriching subjectivity and autonomy on our side.

To understand the task of the militant, we can use Churchill's metaphor of the plague in reference to Lenin. We must hold back the force that spreads the plague in our own body and accelerate the bacteria produced by class struggle in the body of our enemy. There is a relationship between the two movements, but it is never symmetrical, linear in time, or teleological. Conflict must therefore function as a plague in the enemy and as a vaccine for us, a controlled inoculation of poison to reinforce our organism. But often the opposite happens: conflict becomes a plague on our side, the source of useless divisions, and a vaccine for the enemy, namely, for capitalist innovation.

DGL: So we come to the figure of the militant, which you write about in your book *Elogio della militanza* (In praise of militancy). Who is the militant? What is their role and why are they important?

GR: Various answers to this question can be found in what we've already said, because militancy isn't a particular element: it's our point of view, it's our form of life, it is what we are, what we say, what we think. Militants are by definition those who put their whole lives into play. This truth takes on different forms in relation to the historical period, to class composition, and to organizational processes. When at the turn of the millennium militants followed the Anglo-Saxon and American fashion of calling themselves activists, this concession wasn't simply linguistic; it was also structural. They lost their incommensurability with figures such as that of the volunteer, who represented the general interest and so the reproduction of the existent. The militant is a divided subject; they continually produce the "us" and the "them"; they take a position and enforce the taking of sides. They separate in order to recompose their own side. They are primarily a figure of negation, because they refuse the existent and fight to destroy it. Starting from negation, they produce collective ends and new forms of life.

Too often, mainly in difficult phases like this, we hear comrades complaining about the absence of struggles or satisfying themselves with struggles taking place elsewhere. This depression and euphoria mimic those of the financial markets; bubbles of enthusiasm and voyeurism appear and disappear at the speed of a tweet. But historical phases aren't good or bad: they are spaces within and against which we must locate ourselves organizationally. They can't be judged on the basis of our desires but must be fought on the basis of what we need to do. We mustn't fall into the bipolar chronicling of struggles and the lack of them, swaying between the euphoria of the football fan and the depression of the spectator, between an unmotivated sense of defeat and unjustified proclamations of victory. We must free ourselves from this way of thinking if we want to be up to the challenges of the present. The most important phase for the revolutionary militant is precisely when there aren't any struggles. When struggles are already happening, it's too late. We must anticipate in order to organize and to steer, not observe in order to tell and describe. And we should also add that often when there are struggles—we are speaking of the Italian context—putative militants don't know what to make of them because they don't fit into their schemes, and even end up blocking their development. Let's neither depress ourselves by gazing out on a flat horizon or be allured by the waves of a stormy sea; let's try instead to gather the invisible eddies that move beneath the apparent calm. This is today's task, our "what is to be done."

DGL: We now come to the categories forged by "post-operaismo" that, as you have shown, risk leading to the false immediacy of translating technical composition into political composition . . .

GR: We must free ourselves once and for all from the ideology of the "post-," that beginning from the 1980s and 1990s has kept us gripped in the vice of a false choice between those who say nothing will ever be the same again and those who say everything will remain the same. Both are mistaken. Using the conceptual tools of Alquati's *modellone* we can say that on the high levels of reality (those of the accumulation of domination and of capital) nothing has changed; on the intermediate levels of reality there have been significant changes; on the base levels of reality things change very quickly. Research is needed to understand permanency and change, where things change and why, what spaces of antagonistic possibility are opened up. Instead, the ideology of the "post-" claimed there was a new and continually renewable world; this is the world depicted by the rhetoric of innovation, which is in fact the rhetoric of contemporary capitalism, a rhetoric that also organizes the concrete materiality of capitalist counter-revolution.

Some of those who assumed the ideology of the "post-," claiming to be taking up the operaist legacy, imagined the class to be the objective result of the real or supposed transformations of capital (although "class" was a term that was banned for a certain period in a sort of decree imposed by the innovationist apparatus). The issue of class composition and the political processes of counter-subjectivation and transformation were repressed, and along with them the rupture with capital and within class composition. They spoke no longer of a class against itself but of a class that magically becomes autonomous and can be recognized only in its autonomy. We no longer needed a break with capital, but only an exodus from it (and even those who saw themselves as strongly critical of and opposed to Negri sometimes ended up reaching similar conclusions). Although stemming from the refusal of labor, some parts of so-called post-operaismo paradoxically ended up giving life to a sort of immaterial and cognitive "laborism," in which they forgot the fundamental difference between capitalist competences and knowledge on our side, between valorization and self-valorization, between the wealth of accumulation and the wealth of struggles. The problem derives from the idea that an already free cooperation exists, with respect to which capital is only a parasitic agent, and that labor has become "common" (which is something we could agree with only if this "common" is understood to be exploitation and abstract labor commanded by capital).

The term "post-operaismo" was coined in Anglo-Saxon and North American universities in an attempt to capture the power of operaismo, to depoliticize it and abstract it from conflict and class composition, to render it good for academia and the political economy of knowledge, and no longer good for struggles. This then became "Italian Theory," which differentiates itself from "Italian thought." In turn this will become "Critical Italian theory," then "Critical Italian thought," and so on in the bad infinity of a theory that's decoupled from class composition and class struggles, moving from university conferences and lecterns to become solidly embedded in the valorization and reproduction of capital.

The 1980s and 1990s saw an increase in theorizations and analyses later collected under this academic definition of "post-operaismo." These analyses attempted to overturn the annihilating—and complementary—images of the end of History and *pensée unique*. The polemical objective was, and remains, correct, but their practical development was often lacking. Some of these conceptual efforts were problematic from the beginning, for reasons that I touched on briefly before—above all the idea that political composition automatically derives from technical composition; others have been extremely productive and can continue to be so as long as they are rethought within the changes that have taken place in the crisis, and as long as "post-operaismo" is no longer considered to be a comprehensive model. But if we don't start again from the beginning, finding new political instruments, we risk going backward, ossifying categories, transforming them into dogmas, making operaismo into something that it never was, namely, a school and not a movement of thought. Seeing operaismo as a school of thought would open up its entire theoretical and revolutionary system to attack. However irrelevant the academic critiques were, it would move the debate toward defending concepts rather than making them useful for struggles. It would risk dragging everything into political marginality. In a recent political seminar, a comrade rightly noted that young people leave home not when their parents chase them away but when they can't take it anymore. The house of "post-operaismo" is no longer productive for our revolutionary tasks and so we will try to complete that original move that operaismo carried out with respect to Marx: the Machiavellian return to principles, that is, to Marx, against Marxism. Now the task is to return to operaismo against its "post-," or at the very least in a way that is radically critical of that which no longer works, or of that which never worked. If we do that, then we retain what is useful to us, and rethink the roots of the rest.

DGL: For example, given the processes of the stratification and industrialization of labor, is cognitive capitalism still a useful category?

GR: It is better to talk about the "cognitivization of labor" in order to, on the one hand, clearly differentiate it from the obscure category of immaterial labor and, on the other hand, to insist on the process of the global reorganization and hierarchization of the forms of production and exploitation in a period in which knowledge is becoming increasingly central to the accumulation of capital. Thus we avoid slipping into the identification between cognitive labor and subjects defined in a sectorial sense, or rather into an opposition between those who work with their hands and those who work with their minds, and imagining the supposed most advanced point of the technical composition (the knowledge worker) as the most advanced point of struggle. Any idea of a progressive linearity must be fought against: the cognitivization of labor also means the cognitivization of exploitation and measure, and the cognitivization of hierarchies and tasks.

We should stress that the global economic crisis has accelerated the processes of stratification and differentiation that were already taking place in contradictory forms and with different levels of intensity in different sectors and in different parts of the world. Taking up Alquati's line, Salvatore Cominu speaks of the industrialization of cognitive labor: competences, functions, and professionality, previously deemed inseparable from the person and the social cooperation in which they took place, are now subjected to processes of real subsumption within the production of goods and of knowledge, of services and of consumption and reproduction time, and so on. As has always happened in the industrial system, this is simultaneously the expropriation of knowledge and the strengthening of its combined form. But it is a strengthening for capital accumulation, which increases social cooperation while feeding on human capacity, incorporating it into the Marxian automatic system of machines. With the cognitivization of labor, *Homo faber* has become *sapiens* and *Homo sapiens* has become *faber*. At least in part, cognitivization and banalization go hand in hand.

On the basis of Alquati's research on the university in the 1970s, we have used the phrase "living knowledge" (*sapere vivo*) to define the new quality of living labor in a historically determined way, or rather social knowledge's tendential incorporation within living labor. This means not simply pointing out the central role assumed by knowledge and science in contemporary forms of production and accumulation but looking at their socialization and their incarnation in living labor. In the 1970s this socialization came about through struggles, through the refusal of labor, through reappropriation, through workers' autonomy: this was the "social worker" as a political rather than a technical figure. Today, more than forty years on, the relations of force have been inverted: socialization takes place primarily in a forced way, starting from capital's needs. Knowledge is neither good nor neutral in itself, as many on the Left think: it is the fruit of a relationship of production, therefore a relationship of conflict and of force. It is a commodity like others, with its own peculiarities that can be grasped, inverted, and counter-used. In the passage from the "social worker" to the cognitive laborer, the subject was incarnated technically and disincarnated politically. The "social worker" was transformed into an actor of innovation and precariousness. It continued to be social; it stopped being a worker.

It is from this point that we must begin again, within and against the present. Our hypothesis, perhaps overly forced and simplistic, is that in today's crisis the recomposition of the destructured middle class and the hierarchized proletariat in the process of the "cognitivization" and reproduction of active human capacity could be the functional equivalent of the alliance between workers and peasants in the crisis of the First World War. We say "it could be" obviously because whether it is or not depends on us, on a potential us, on an us that isn't limited to what we currently are. If we don't have the capacity to recompose ourselves, the middle class and the proletariat will be susceptible to reactionary alternatives, or at least they will reproduce themselves as fragments created by the government of the crisis. Today more than ever we must move within the ambiguity of the process with a unilateral point of view, with extreme tactical flexibility and a tough strategic rigidity: better the messiness of the real than the purity of ideology, better to dispute the social territories of the conflictual materialist Right than to take up preaching with the faint-hearted idealist Left, better the problems of militant coresearch than the useless certainty of activist selfies. To use the words of the poet, "Where there is danger / A rescuing element grows as well."[7]

DGL: More than a hundred years have now passed since the Russian Revolution. In what way did operaismo in the 1970s use

Lenin and how can reflecting on the Leninist experience still be useful today?

GR: When a terrified Churchill described Lenin as a plague bacillus transported in a sealed German truck, he involuntarily supplied us with an extraordinary definition of what revolutionary militants are: bacteria carrying the plague. And Lenin committed himself to organizing this plague. Marx showed us the mechanisms of the capitalist machine; the question—which would return in operaismo, and which we must keep in mind in our militant practice—is how not to remain trapped in this mechanism, how to break the closed circle. Where to hit it, how to spread the plague, in what way and at what points we can destroy the enemy, starting not from the laws of the movement of capital but from the laws of the movement of the working class within and against capitalist society. This is where we see both Lenin's continuity with, and his overturning of, Marx.

The historicist and objectivist Lenin faithful to stages of development that has been handed down to us by Leninism is a complete misrepresentation and must be abandoned. Throughout his life Lenin continually tried to force, interrupt, and overturn the development of capital, or rather to impose revolutionary will within and against history. In his debates with the Russian populists, Lenin didn't say that the development of capitalism in Russia was necessary and desirable; he said simply that it was a fact. The battle carried out by the revolutionary Narodniks was lost; the war remained to be fought. Given this they needed to look for new forms of expression of revolutionary subjectivity and build adequate forms of organization. This is Lenin's wager: the industrial proletariat, although seen as being in a "corner" by the populists of his day (who had betrayed the legacy of revolutionary populism), were, in tendency, the front line, "the vanguard of the whole mass of toilers and exploited."[8] Is this tendency destined to be realized thanks to the inevitable laws of the movement of capital? Of course not: only the struggle decides destiny. Everything else remains imprisoned in managing the false certainties of the present. We need to choose, we need to make a wager, we need to dare: "Whoever wants to depict some living phenomenon in its development is inevitably and necessarily confronted with the dilemma of either running ahead or lagging behind."[9] There is no middle way, he argued. That was the case in 1905 and again in February 1917; it is only the "tail-ists" who could think those were bourgeois revolutions and that the proletarians had to wait their turn, had to wait for historical development to hand them socialism and then communism rather than struggling for them. This is nonsense! We need to be within the revolutionary movement, break its linearity, steer it toward other ends. We need to leap over the stages of development, launch the potential of the possible against the misery of the objective. This is the only way to have a revolution against Marx's *Capital*, breaking his vicious circle.

The most significant lesson Lenin taught us was that revolutionaries must be prepared for every opportunity, without thinking that they will fall from the sky and transcend the materiality of historical dynamics, organizational continuity, and the patient construction of relations of force. We must methodically create the conditions of possibility to seize the opportunity, to grab the lightning bolt with our bare hands. This is about rethinking the relationship between process and event, or rather duration and leap, in a completely different way: for the simple continuity of the process without the discontinuity of the event leads to objectivism, while the pure discontinuity of the event without the continuity of the process leads to idealism. This is how the Bolshevik leader took the will inherited from the revolutionary populists and stood it on the legs of historical materialism, extracting the historical materialism of Marx from the iron cage of objectivism.

If we need to forget the Lenin of the Leninists, we also need to forget the Lenin of the anti-Leninists, which in the end amounts to the same thing. Because both reduce him to something he never was, a gray functionary of organization. They forget that in his organization Lenin was almost always a minority, because ultimately a revolutionary always takes a minority line: a minority that isn't minoritarian, that isn't the ideology and representation of a marginal identity, but instead has a hegemonic vocation. "Should we dream?" he imagines asking the party's central committee, to which he replies, yes, because when there is a rift between dreams and reality, when you act materialistically and work conscientiously to realize those dreams, when "there is some connection between dreams and life, then all is well. Of this kind of dreaming there is unfortunately too little in our movement."[10] Just as then, so today, we need to rediscover our ability to dream and to give organized form to that dream. Notwithstanding the evolutionist Leninists and those who call themselves anti-Leninists, this is the main lesson of Lenin's "What Is to Be Done?" And this is the Lenin who—in a sort of Alquatianism *ante litteram*—continually critiques the cult of spontaneity as much as the fetish of organization. Spontaneity isn't always good and isn't always bad; there are moments in which it is advanced and moments in which it falls behind. In periods of struggle or insurrection, often it is spontaneity that imposes an offensive terrain while organization falls behind and needs to be rethought at that level, on that terrain. In other periods spontaneity disappears or is shaped by the order of discourse of the enemy. Then, organization must reopen paths to its antagonistic development.

This is more or less the Lenin who, in different ways, emerged from the better bits of operaismo (we recommend, for instance, *Factory of Strategy: 33 Lessons on Lenin* by Negri). But their important attempt to take Lenin's method beyond Lenin was limited by the fact that it wasn't accompanied by an adequate plan of organizational reinvention. It often ended up repeating something that couldn't be repeated, that is, the specific solutions given by Lenin. And when faced with their inevitable failure, there was a repression of the still relevant problems that Lenin had posed regarding the mutable relationship between class composition and forms of revolutionary organization.

DGL: A final question: In what way should we study the past to modify the present or, put differently, produce theory with the aim of organizing struggles?

GR: Following on from what we were saying, let's make one thing clear: the past never tells us what to do in the present. It shows us errors not to be repeated, limits to overcome, a richness to reinvent. It sends us questions, not answers. And it tells us what we must take revenge for. But how can this be done? This question is asked by every generation of militants. If we want to take on a political legacy, we shouldn't celebrate it, transforming it into an empty testimony; we must set it alight, transform it into a weapon against the present. Otherwise, it's useless. Operaismo, Marx, and Lenin are for us a partisan political style and a political method. They are not those represented in academic philology nor by the "post-operaist" Marxist and Leninist catechism—these can be abandoned without shedding a tear. The problem for militants is to appropriate tradition without reverential cults and without hypostasizing it: rethinking its richness, criticizing its limits, discarding that which is no longer useful. That's what Lenin did with Marx (and also the revolutionary populists), and that's what the operaisti did with Marx and Lenin. And, at the same time, we must take up what is useful in the thought of our enemies: as Tronti said, better a great reactionary than a small revolutionary.

That's why it's a problem that at the international level operaismo has been reduced to so-called post-operaismo, and largely to the Negri of *Empire*. We are not interested in questions of intellectual property or of branding—we leave the copyright disputes to the family members of the deceased. What is interesting for us is political usefulness. And it is precisely this reduction of operaismo that deprives many militants of the possibility of exploring the submerged Atlantis of figures like Alquati and thus of finding weapons that are today completely indispensable.

The revolutionary method of operaismo taught us that we need to study that which we want to destroy: capitalism, and the capital that is within us. Those who fall in love with the object of their analysis, in order to reproduce the roles they have acquired within this society, abandon militancy and pass into the enemy camp. It's not even worth calling it betrayal; it is simply their incapacity to break with the separateness of their own condition. Those who choose the individual path will die alone. That which distinguishes militants is the hatred for that which they study. The militant needs hatred to produce knowledge. A lot of hatred, studying the core of that which they hate most. Militant creativity is above all the science of destruction. So political practice either is pregnant with theory or it isn't political practice. We need to study in order to act, we need to act in order to study. And to do the two things together. Now more than ever, this is our political task.

And we need to teach ourselves to create political methods: it is here that counter-subjectivity is produced in a real rather than ephemeral way, adopting a way of thinking and reasoning that is not standardized (how much conformism there is in the theoretical and practical fields of the so-called movement!), capable therefore of autonomously constructing responses adapted to different situations, of flexibly modifying hypotheses and behaviors beginning from the rigidity of collective ends. The task of autonomous *formazione* is to create a common method of reasoning, as well as a transformation and questioning of the specific procedures through which this method is expressed. This can't be entrusted simply to individuals but must be organized collectively.

Formazione for what? To rediscover the power of the wager. A materialist wager, a revolutionary wager. A wager on the possibility of transforming the capitalist crisis into a revolutionary crisis, and even before that, of transforming the crisis of political subjectivity into an urgently needed leap forward. To ape that which was there before would be grotesque. Instead, we need to study it, to turn it toward our current problems. Autonomy is the constant readiness to subvert what we are, with the aim of destroying and overturning the existent. It is the construction of a collective perspective of force and possibility beginning from the radical liberation and transformation of the elements that make up the present. This is why autonomy lives in the revolutionary method, not in the slogans of radical merchandising. We need to dare to make a wager, dare to act, dare to have a revolution. After all, isn't this what we live for?

Notes

Chapter 1

1. Translator's note: In order to distinguish Italian operaismo from other workerisms, the Italian word "operaismo" will be used throughout the text, with the anglicization "operaist" as its adjective. Those involved in operaismo will be referred to using the Italian word "operaisti." The word "operaietà" will remain in Italian, and describes the subjectivity of the figure around which the working class is politically recomposed.

2. For further information on the German experience we recommend the book *La rivoluzione tedesca 1918–1919*, with a preface by Sergio Bologna, and Bologna's essay, "Composizione di classe e teoria del partito alle origini del movimento consiliare" (Class composition and the theory of the party at the origins of the councilist movement) published in *Operai e stato*, which came out in 1972 as part of the series "Materiali marxisti" published by Feltrinelli and edited by comrades at the Institute of Political Sciences in Padua.

3. Published in C. L. R. James, *You Don't Play with Revolution: The Montréal Lectures of CLR James*, ed. David Austin (Edinburgh: AK Press, 2009).

4. On this we recommend Negri's article "Lenin e i soviet nella rivoluzione" (Lenin and the soviets in the revolution) published in 1965 in the first edition of *Classe operaia* and translated as "The Factory of Strategy" in his book *Factory of Strategy: Thirty-Three Lessons on Lenin* (New York: Columbia University Press, 2014). In this book we also find the formula "organization is spontaneity reflecting upon itself," which closely echoes Romano Alquati's definition of "organized spontaneity," which he used to interpret the struggles in Turin at the beginning of the 1960s, and to which we will return later.

5. On this subject we recommend Rita di Leo's *L'esperimento profano* (Rome: Ediesse, 2012).

6. The Federazione Italiana Operai Metallurgici (Fiom) is the metalwork sector of the Confederazione Generale Italiana del Lavoro (CGIL), the trade union linked to the Communist Party.

7. Olivetti is a historic business based in Ivrea in the province of Turin, which started off by manufacturing typewriters. After the Second World War, businessman and intellectual Adriano Olivetti, bringing together elements of Fabianism and humanitarian and Christian socialism, developed the idea of a utopian community that would be both productive and harmonious, able to guarantee the development of society and the individual. His Movimento Comunità (Community Movement) stood for election and, more importantly, attracted many intellectuals, trade unionists, and experts who wanted to set up an innovative industry based on the concept of a capitalism founded on technical progress and interclass harmony. While the Left, past and present, is lavish in its praise of the Olivettian "community," Alquati saw it as a mystification, revealing the antagonistic reality and organized conflict within it. This partly explains both his problems with the Left and why he is remembered as a lonely and isolated figure.

8. On alienation in the Taylorist factory, and especially on the worker who embodies it, with all their ambivalences and potential for struggle, György Lukács's classic *History and Class Consciousness* is essential reading.

9. We capitalize the word "History" when it is understood as a necessary teleological progression, which for the apologists of the current system ended with the triumph of capital, and for Marxists will evolve into socialism and, ultimately, communism.

10. Mario Tronti, "Rileggendo 'La libertà comunista,'" in *Galvano Della Volpe. Un altro marxismo*, ed. Guido Liguori (Rome: Fahrenheit 451, 2000), 14.

11. For more in-depth discussions on this topic, see Gigi Roggero, Guido Borio, and Francesca Pozzi, *Futuro anteriore* (Rome: DeriveApprodi, 2002).

12. See the interview with Alquati in *Futuro anteriore*. This, like the other interviews mentioned below, are all on the CD-ROM that comes with the book; some parts of the interviews were then published in *Gli operaisti*, edited by Gigi Roggero, Guido Borio, and Francesca Pozzi (Rome: DeriveApprodi, 2005).

13. The *magliette a strisce* ("striped T-shirts"), in reference to the fashion at the time for striped cotton T-shirts in bright colors, was the nickname given to the young people who took to the streets in June and July 1960 against the congress of the neo-fascist party, Movimento Sociale Italiano. In June of that year, with the authorization of Tambroni's Christian Democratic government, the party had announced that its congress would be held in Genoa, which was considered the capital of the Resistance. On June 30, people in Genoa took to the streets in protest, engaging in intense clashes with the police, which led to the cancellation of the congress. In the following days the protests spread to other

Italian cities, and a number of demonstrators were killed by the police. The most important thing about this movement in Genoa is not so much, or at least not only, its expression of mass antifascism, but above all the emergence of a new class composition, largely made up of young workers and proletarians.

14. In July 1962, in Piazza Statuto in Turin, young workers assaulted the headquarters of a union responsible for signing a contract that favored the bosses.

Chapter 2

1. Mario Tronti, "A New Type of Political Experiment: Lenin in England," in *Workers and Capital*, trans. David Broder (London: Verso, 2019), 65.

2. Tronti's essay "Tra materialismo dialettico e filosofia della prassi. Gramsci e Labriola" (Between dialectical materialism and the philosophy of Praxis: Gramsci and Labriola) was published that year in the book *La città futura*, edited by Caracciolo and Scalia (Milan: Feltrinelli, 1959).

3. Tronti, "Tra materialismo dialettico e filosofia della prassi," 153.

4. Tronti, "Tra materialismo dialettico e filosofia della prassi," 155.

5. Tronti, "Tra materialismo dialettico e filosofia della prassi," 155.

6. Romano Alquati, *Sulla FIAT e altri scritti* (Milan: Feltrinelli, 1975), 52.

7. Alquati, *Sulla FIAT e altri scritti*, 51–52.

8. "Non garantiti" was a label given to workers without permanent contracts, a condition that was often also a personal choice, and which in the following decades would come to be known as "precarious" or "flexible" work. For more on the "non garantiti," see Alberto Asor Rosa's book, *Le due società. Ipotesi sulla crisi italiana* (Turin: Einaudi, 1977).

9. Translator's note: There is no simple English translation for the word *formazione*, which is more specific than the English word "formation" and broader than the English word "education." In Italy, *educazione* is the transmission of already existing behaviors, values, and discipline—so much so that you say *buona educazione* to mean politeness, a respect for the rules of society, while *formazione* is an open process of construction of the capacity for reasoning, knowledge, and the creation of a point of view, at times describing something more like the "formation" of a subject.

10. This is taken from *Camminando per realizzare un sogno comune* (Turin: Velleità Alternative, 1994), 22.

11. See Steve Wright, *Storming Heaven: Class Composition and Struggle in Italian Autonomist Marxism* (London: Pluto Press, 2017). There are some other texts worth reading on this issue: Maria Grazia Meriggi's *Composizione di classe e teoria del partito* (Class composition and the theory of the party), published in 1978 by Dedalo as a collection of essays, almost all of which had previously appeared in *Aut aut*; and Sergio Bologna's lecture on class composition organized by Commonware in Bologna in 2012 and available in the book *Geneaologie del futuro*. If you want to read the original documents, among Alquati's many texts, we particularly recommend the two parts of the article "Composizione organica del capitale e forza-lavoro alla Olivetti" ("Organic composition of capital and labor-power at Olivetti" [*Viewpoint Magazine*, September 27, 2013]), in the second and third issues of *Quaderni rossi*, and also *Sacre icone* (Sacred icons), written and published in 1993 by Calusca.

12. The idea of "going to the people" comes from populist militant intellectuals in Russia in the second half of the nineteenth century.

13. Alquati, *Sulla FIAT e altri scritti*, 57, 64.

14. Alquati, *Sulla FIAT e altri scritti*, 64.

15. It is important to distinguish between spontaneism and spontaneity. Spontaneity is part of the behavior of class struggle; spontaneism is the ideologization of spontaneity.

16. Alquati, *Sulla FIAT e altri scritti*, 65.

17. Alquati, *Sulla FIAT e altri scritti*, 51.

18. This is elaborated on in Federico Chicchi and Salvatore Cominu's lecture on coresearch, published in *Genealogie del futuro* (Verona: Ombre Corte, 2013), which very clearly explains the different role of temporality in Panzieri and Alquati.

19. In *L'operaismo degli anni Sessanta. Dai "Quaderni rossi" a "Classe operaia,"* edited by Giuseppe Trotta and Fabio Milana (Rome: DeriveApprodi, 2008), 738.

Chapter 3

1. More can be found on this tension and conflict in the fourth part of Alquati's book, *Camminando per realizzare un sogno comune* (Walking to realize a common dream), entitled "Su Montaldi (Panzieri, io) e la conricerca" (On Montaldi (Panzieri and me) and coresearch). We'd also recommend *Com'eri bella classe operaia* (How beautiful the working class was) by Romolo Gobbi (Milan:

Longanesi, 1989), which contains some brilliant anecdotes. Indeed, it is often easier to understand the subjectivity of the people involved from books like these than from disembodied theoretical analyses.

2. See the interview with Alquati in *Futuro anteriore*.

3. See Luciano Bianciardi's reflections on this subject in *Il lavoro culturale* (Milan: Feltrinelli, 1957) and *La vita agra* (Milan: Rizzoli, 1962), and the film *Chi lavora è perduto* (Who works is lost) by Tinto Brass, which in 1963 had already raised the question of the refusal of labor through the story of a failed worker in the culture industry in Veneto, which had been transformed by unbridled processes of factory-ization. ("Factory-ization" is a term used particularly by Alquati to describe the process of the extension of the factory to the whole of society.)

4. Alquati, *Sulla FIAT e altri scritti*, 65.

5. You will find this and other texts by Asor Rosa in the collection *Le armi della critica* (Turin: Giulio Einaudi editore, 2011), 17.

6. Mario Tronti, "Marx Yesterday and Today," in *Workers and Capital*, trans. David Broder (London: Verso, 2019), 7.

7. Tronti, "Marx Yesterday and Today," 10.

8. Mario Tronti, "A Course of Action," in *Workers and Capital*, trans. David Broder (London: Verso, 2019), xviii.

9. Tronti, "A Course of Action," xviii.

10. Tronti, "A Course of Action," xxviii.

11. Tronti, "A Course of Action," xxiii.

12. Mario Tronti, "The Class" in *Workers and Capital*, trans. David Broder (London: Verso, 2019), 233–234.

13. Tronti, "A Course of Action," xviii.

14. Mario Tronti, "Introduzione," in Karl Marx, *Scritti inediti di economia politica* (Rome: Editori Riuniti, 1963), xxxv.

15. Tronti, "Introduzione," xxxvi.

16. Tronti, "A Course of Action," xxiii.

17. Asor Rosa, *Le armi della critica*, xli–xlii.

18. Asor Rosa, *Le armi della critica*, xlii.

19. See the interview with Alquati in *Futuro anteriore*.

20. *Politicità*—literally, "politicalness"—is the political character of a behavior that according to Alquati can be either intrinsic or extrinsic.

21. In *The Man without Qualities* (New York: Vintage Books, 1996), Robert Musil distinguished between passive passivity and the active passivity of a "prisoner waiting for his chance to break out" (386).

22. Mario Tronti, "Factory and Society," in *Workers and Capital*, trans. David Broder (London: Verso, 2019), 31.

23. Tronti, "A Course of Action," xxxiii.

24. Tronti, "A Course of Action," xix.

25. Romano Alquati, "Struggle at Fiat" (1964), trans. Evan Calder Williams (*Viewpoint Magazine*, September 26, 2013), https://viewpointmag.com/2013/09/26/struggle-at-fiat-1964/.

26. Alquati, "Struggle at Fiat."

27. Alquati, "Struggle at Fiat" (translation modified).

28. Alquati, *Sulla FIAT e altri scritti*, 49.

29. We recommend the part of Negri's autobiography *Storia di un comunista* (History of a communist) devoted to the 1960s, in which he analyzes the characteristics and peculiarities of the intervention at Porto Marghera and its relationship with the operaist experience. In *Quando il potere è operaio* (When power is workers' power) (Rome: Manifestolibri, 2009), Gianni Sbrogiò and Devi Sacchetto carefully reconstruct the experience of the Assemblea Autonoma at Porto Marghera through essays and testimonies. It's also worth reading *Sul sindacato e altri scritti* (On the union and other writings) by Guido Bianchini (Padua: Quaderni del Progetto, 1990), who wrote very few "official" texts, despite his extraordinary political intelligence and sophisticated theoretical and political insight, which was crucial to the *formazione* of the young militants. See also Giovanni Giovannelli and Gianni Sbrogiò, eds., *Guido Bianchini. Ritratto di un maestro dell'operaismo* (Rome: DeriveApprodi, 2021).

30. Tronti, "A New Type of Political Experiment: Lenin in England," 65.

31. Tronti, "A Course of Action," xxx.

32. Tronti, "Factory and Society," 26.

33. Interview with Tronti in *Futuro anteriore*. On this subject, we recommend Gaspare De Caro and Enzo Grillo's typewritten text, circulated in 1973 in groups linked to Potere Operaio and now difficult to get hold of, "L'esperienza storica della rivista Classe Operaia" (The historical experience of the newspaper *Classe operaia*). Written a few years after its end, it thoroughly analyzes the ambiguities and unresolved problems in the newspaper's history.

34. "Classepartitoclasse," in *Classe operaia* (March 1967), 1.

35. "Classepartitoclasse," 1.

Chapter 4

1. For more on this, see both his interview in *Futuro anteriore* and his introduction to the book *L'operaismo degli anni sessanta*, which has also been published separately as *Noi operaisti* (Rome: DeriveApprodi, 2009).

2. This 1979 edition was published by Macchina Libri. The argument is further developed in his interview on operaismo of the same year with Paolo Pozzi and Roberta Tommasini, *Dall'operaio massa all'operaio sociale* (From the mass worker to the social worker) (Milan: Multhipla edizioni, 1979).

3. Reprinted by DeriveApprodi: *Maggio '68 in Francia* (Rome: DeriveApprodi, 2008).

4. He elaborated on this in another text written with Francesco Ciafaloni, "I tecnici come produttori e come prodotto" (Technicians as producers and product), published in March 1969 in *Quaderni piacentini*. Potere Operaio also reflected politically on this subject: they published an article on the struggles of technicians at a factory in Rome in the 1969 issue of *La classe*; and one of their four pamphlets published between 1969 and 1970, entitled "Linea di massa" (Mass line) is entirely devoted to technicians (the other three being about Snam Progetti, the school system, and Porto Marghera).

5. By this we mean the appropriation not only of a wage but also of an "indirect" income in terms of services (for example, houses, transport, and general consumption).

6. See the interview with Dalmaviva in *Futuro anteriore*.

7. Shakespeare, *Henry IV Part 1*, act 5, scene 2.

8. Antonio Negri, "Keynes and the Capitalist Theory of the State Post-1929," in *Revolution Retrieved: Writings on Marx, Keynes, Capitalist Crisis and New Social Subjects (1967–1983)* (London: Red Notes, 1988); Antonio Negri, "Marx on Cycle and Crisis," in *Revolution Retrieved: Writings on Marx, Keynes, Capitalist Crisis and New Social Subjects (1967–1983)* (London: Red Notes, 1988).

9. See Marco Scavino, *Potere operaio* (Rome: DeriveApprodi, 2018).

10. In March 1973, there was an occupation of the FIAT Mirafiori factory in Turin, which was a symbol of Italian industry and workers' struggles in the 1960s. Coming at the height of an all-out strike and of daily internal demonstrations that "swept" the bosses and scabs away from the workshops, the occupation was organized autonomously from the unions and also from the revolutionary groups. The occupation's principal protagonist was the very combative new generation of workers, who expressed a generalized refusal of work. Their nickname comes from the red handkerchiefs they wore around their necks.

11. For further readings on this subject, see the lengthy analysis and inquiry in "Issue Zero" of *Controinformazione*, October 1973.

12. Karl Heinz Roth, *L'altro movimento operaio* (The other workers' movement) (Milan: Feltrinelli, 1976). Materiali marxisti was a series of books published by Feltrinelli, first edited by Sergio Bologna and Toni Negri, and then by the Political Science Collective at the University of Padua.

13. On this link, see the interviews with Ferruccio Gambino and Bruno Cartosio in *Futuro anteriore*.

14. Between April 1970 and May–June 1971 two issues of *Compagni*, (Comrades,) were published, a journal promoted by Potere Operaio and led by Nanni Balestrini, which encouraged reflection on international movements.

15. For more on this, see Anna Curcio's "Marxist Feminism of Rupture" (*Viewpoint Magazine*, January 24, 2020).

16. In the summer of 1970, the capital of the region of Calabria in Southern Italy was moved from Catanzaro to Reggio Calabria: this set off violent riots that would last for some time. It was a real popular revolt in response to various issues, above all the malaise of Southern Italian cities. The Left, which was incapable of understanding the material roots of the riot, branded it as fascist due to the right-wing groups that took advantage of the almost complete absence of other organizations.

17. It would be helpful to reflect historically on the ambivalences of *diciannovismo* and on the incapacity of the revolutionary forces to turn it in the opposite direction, but, unfortunately, we don't have space to do that here.

18. For a general outline and a more in-depth analysis of this, see *Gli autonomi*, edited by DeriveApprodi, of which twelve volumes have been published since 2007. It discusses the history of Autonomia in Italy, detailing the different experiences in the various regions.

19. See the interview with Tronti in *Futuro anteriore*.

20. *Il manifesto* was founded in 1969 as the monthly political newspaper of a left-wing component of the Italian Communist Party. As the paper went against the official line of the party (in particular on the Soviet invasion of Prague), this component was expelled from the party in November 1969. It then also became an institutional political group that had modest election results. In 1971 *Il manifesto* became a daily paper.

21. The Collettivi Politici Veneti were a network of all the autonomist political organizations in Veneto, mainly coming out of the experience of Potere Operaio.

22. On this, see the fifth volume of *Gli autonomi*, written by Donato Tagliapietra: *L'autonomia operaia vicentina. Dalla rivolta di Valdagno alla repressione di Thiene*

(The Autonomia Operaia of Vicenza: From the Valdagno revolt to the Thiene repression) (Rome: DeriveApprodi, 2019). He links the experiences of the Venetian political collectives to the passage from the mass worker to the social worker and to new practices of organization, struggle, and the use of force, founded on the refusal of work, mass illegality, and the creation of counter-power.

23. Collaborators included Dalmaviva, Daghini, Scalzone, Lauso Zagato, Paolo Virno, Alberto Magnaghi, and Paolo Benvegnù. The editorial written by Piperno is particularly significant: "Da Potere operaio a Linea di condotta" (From Potere Operaio to *Linea di condotta*), July–October 1975.

24. To get an idea of the radicality and foresight of Bifo's hypothesis, we recommend *Quarant'anni contro il lavoro* (Forty years against work) (Rome: DeriveApprodi, 2017), which collects various articles from that period.

25. This summary is not exhaustive. For example, there were journals such as *Quaderni del territorio* (Notebooks on the territory), linked to political valorization and the capacity to read the tendency, which also used the skills learned in the academic environment. See *"Quaderni del Territorio." Dalla città fabbrica alla città digitale. Saggi e ricerche (1976–1981)*, edited by Alberto Magnaghi (Rome: DeriveApprodi, 2021).

26. See the already cited interview on operaismo in *Dall'operaio massa all'operaio sociale*.

27. Romano Alquati, "Ulteriori note sull'università e il territorio," in Romano Alquati, Nicola Negri, Andrea Sormano, *Università di ceto medio e proletariato intellettuale* (Turin: Stampatori, 1978), 33.

28. Alquati, "Ulteriori note sull'università e il terrirorio," 116.

29. Alquati, "Ulteriori note sull'università e il terrirorio," 91.

30. Romano Alquati, "L'Università e la formazione," *Aut aut*, no. 154 (July–August 1976), 96.

31. Antonio Negri, *Factory of Strategy: Thirty-Three Lessons on Lenin*, trans. Arianna Bove (New York: Columbia University Press, 2014), 59–60.

Chapter 5

1. For a more in-depth analysis of this, see his interviews in *Futuro anteriore*. See also "Su Montaldi (Panzieri, io) e la conricerca" (On Montaldi (Panzieri, me) and coresearch) in *Camminando per realizzare un sogno comune*. On Alquati's political and intellectual biography, see also *Un cane in chiesa* (Rome: DeriveApprodi, 2020) edited by Francesco Bedani and Francesca Ioannilli.

2. An Italian state school with a focus on the humanities.

3. The Confederazione Italiana Sindacati Lavoratori (CISL) is a trade union that was linked to Democrazia Cristiana, the former Christian Democratic party that governed Italy in the postwar period up until the beginning of the 1990s.

4. On the theme of coresearch, see *Per fare conricerca* (How to do coresearch) (Rome: DeriveApprodi, 2022) and "Di nuovo sulla conricerca e precisazioni sulla conricerca" (Again on coresearch and clarifications of coresearch), in *Camminando per realizzare un sogno comune*.

5. The texts of the research "Sulla riproduzione della capacità umana vivente" (On the reproduction of living human capacity) from 2002 have been published under the same name by DeriveApprodi (2021). The text "Nella società industriale d'oggi" (In today's industrial society) from 2001 is also due to be published by DeriveApprodi.

6. Alquati believed there were different moments of research, distinguished according to the aims of the research and those carrying it out. Thus coresearch is the construction of a particular form of knowledge for struggle, for recomposition, and for the planning of conflict. Coresearch has a certain continuity, and is rooted in social reality. But there are other forms of research and study that have different locations: inquiry at a lower level allows for the more impromptu knowledge of a particular phenomenon or situation; the production of theoretical synthesis takes place at a higher level and in different contexts and is the result of an analysis with a more complex outlook. All of these forms of knowledge construction can and must interact through processes of communication and mutual reinforcement.

7. Alquati's general model of how capitalist civilization is redefined in the neomodern phase of hyperindustriality was presented and developed for the first time in *Dispense di sociologia industriale* (Handouts on industrial sociology), volume 3, parts I and II (Turin: Il Segnalibro editore, 1989).

8. His research on *formazione* was first summarized in *Introduzione a un modello sulla formazione* (Introduction to a model of *formazione*), volume 4, part I (Turin: Il Segnalibro editore, 1992).

9. Alquati distinguishes between the strengthening of capacities aimed at the development of capitalism and the enrichment of capacities aimed at the autonomous development of human capacity. According to Alquati, they do not always go hand in hand. On the contrary, today we are seeing a strengthening of the former through an impoverishment of the latter.

10. At the beginning of the 1990s, Alquati focused on what was happening in the universities and, as a professor, closely observed the Pantera movement. Some

of his reflections are collected in *Cultura, formazione, ricerca: Industrializzazione della produzione immateriale* (Culture, *formazione*, research: The industrialization of immaterial production) (Turin: Velleità alternative, 1994).

11. In 1992 a small group was formed in Turin with the aim of carrying out coresearch. Alquati participated in some of its activities, and his contribution can be found in *Sul comunicare* (On communicating) (Turin: Il Segnalibro editore, 1993).

12. Science was a key interest for Alquati, and he dedicated much analysis and research to it between the 1970s and the 1990s. However, his texts are fragmentary. They can be found in *Dispense di sociologia industriale, Nella società industriale d'oggi*, and *Camminando per realizzare un sogno comune*. But a 1970s collection for internal use entitled *La merce scienza* (The science commodity) has been lost. Only some incomplete typescripts remain, which were part of a talk given at a conference at the University of Calabria in which Alfred Sohn-Rethel also participated.

13. In the same period there was a special issue of *Aut aut* (no. 154, 1976) dedicated to research on the class composition of university students entitled *L'università e la formazione. L'incorporamento del sapere sociale nel lavoro vivo*.

14. On the dichotomy between classes, see *Sacre icone. Le classi esistono ancora?* (Sacred icons: Do classes still exist?) (Padua: Calusca, 1993), and some parts of *Dispense di sociologia industriale* and *Nella società industriale d'oggi*.

15. Romano Alquati, *Dispense di Sociologia Industriale* (Turin: Il Segnalibro, 1989), Part III, Books 1–2.

16. This research can be found in *Sulla riproduzione della capacità umana vivente*.

17. Some reflections on this can be found in *Sul virtuale* (On the virtual), written with Maurizio Pentenero and Jean-Louis Weissberg (Turin: Velleità alternative, 1994).

18. An initial part of these analyses was published in *Lavoro e attività. Per un'analisi della schiavitù neomoderna* (Labor and activity: Toward an analysis of neo-modern slavery) (Rome: manifestolibri, 1997), while other writings on labor are still unpublished.

19. At the beginning of the 1980s, Alquati carried out research on women, family, and the service sector in the province of Cremona with Giovanni Lodi, which was then published in 1981 by the Provincial Government of Cremona with the title *Donna, famiglia, servizi nel territorio della provincia di Cremona* (Women, family and services in the province of Cremona) (Cremona: Amministrazione provinciale, 1981). At the end of the 1990s he followed Francesca Pozzi in

researching the subjectivity of feminist militants, although that research was never published.

Chapter 6

1. Giorgio Agamben et al., *Sentimenti dell'aldiqua* (Rome: Theoria, 1990).

2. For those who want to delve more deeply into this subject, as well as reading *Grundrisse*, we also recommend *Genesi e struttura del "Capitale" di Marx* (Genesis and structure of Marx's *Capital*) by Roman Rosdolsky (Rome-Bari: Laterza, 1971) and *Marx beyond Marx* by Negri (New York: Autonomedia, 1991).

3. Karl Marx, *Grundrisse: Foundations of Political Economy*, trans. Martin Nicolaus (London: Penguin Books, 1993), 693.

4. Marx, *Grundrisse*, 693.

5. Marx, *Grundrisse*, 692.

6. Marx, *Grundrisse*, 706.

7. Marx, *Grundrisse*, 704–705.

8. Tronti, "A Course of Action," xxii.

9. Tronti, "A Course of Action," xxvi–xxvii.

10. Marx, *Grundrisse*, 700.

11. Marx, *Grundrisse*, 706.

12. A brief clarification: refusing nostalgia doesn't mean refusing the past or refusing tradition. We must appropriate the past, with all its riches and its limits, to use its inheritance and to construct our own tradition. Tradition isn't about gazing on the ashes of the past or hoping for some utopian future: it is a weapon to be continually produced and reinvented in the present. It isn't handed to us objectively by the passing of time, but, on the contrary, must be subjectively won through our ability to interrupt it.

13. Tronti, "A Course of Action," xxvii–xxviii.

14. *UniNomade* texts can be found in the archive of uninomade.org. It is also worth noting that an international network was created around the group and the political experiences that preceded it, including particularly stable contacts with Spain, France, and Brazil, and relationships with different figures in other parts of the world such as North America.

15. Alquati, *Sulla FIAT e altri scritti*, 65.

16. Interview with Tronti in *Futuro anteriore*.

17. Since the beginning of the 1990s some important analyses have been written about the crisis and financialization processes, in particular those by Christian Marazzi—most recently in *Il comunismo del capitale* (The communism of capital) (Verona: Ombre Corte, 2010) and the *Diario della crisi infinita* (Diary of the infinite crisis) (Verona: Ombre Corte, 2015). Our insistence on the limits of this period doesn't at all mean we want to ignore the wealth of analysis in recent decades—on the contrary, we hope to save it.

18. Mario Tronti, *Con le spalle al futuro* (Rome: Editori Riuniti, 1992), 39.

19. Tronti, "A Course of Action," xxx.

20. Mario Tronti, *Dello spirito libero* (Milan: Il Saggiatore, 2015), 86.

21. Tronti, "The Class," 240.

Appendix

1. This appendix is a slightly edited version of the original interview in order to avoid repetition with the rest of the book. This version also appeared in English in *Viewpoint Magazine* (viewpointmag.com). The full Italian version of this interview was published on Commonware (commonware.org) and the full French version on Période (revueperiode.net).

2. Tronti, "The Class," 233–234.

3. Mario Tronti, "What the Proletariat Is," in *Workers and Capital*, trans. David Broder (London: Verso, 2019), 194

4. Mario Tronti, "The Plan of Capital," in *Workers and Capital*, trans. David Broder (London: Verso, 2019), 57.

5. The concept of "levels of reality" is a reference to Alquati's model, his synthesis of the capitalist system. This system is organized hierarchically according to different levels of reality: on the high levels we have the accumulation of domination and capital, the macro-ends of the system, and on the base levels we have the daily functioning of the system in its immediate and concrete expressions. All of this hinges on the medium level, where we have activity, transformed into labor. This model isn't a simple summary of the existent, and neither is it structuralist; it is, rather, Alquati's attempt to synthesize the processes through which the whole capitalist system functions, to be able to identify its different dynamics, its ambivalences, and its contradictions, thus the possibilities of conflict and of counter-subjectivity, of rupture and liberation. To speak of levels from the point of view of the forms of antagonistic organization doesn't mean imagining a simple overturning of the dialectic of the capitalist model, or reproposing a symmetry between technical composition and political composition. It instead means attempting to call into question the capitalist hierarchy without limiting ourselves to a sterile testimony of a horizontalist ideology. In a system of social relations that are vertically hierarchical, horizontality is always what is at stake in conflict, never its starting point. The medium range—situated between the levels of abstraction above and the levels of reality below—is the place in which it is possible to consolidate processes of counter-subjectivity, ensuring struggles at the base affect the high levels. For this reason, it is the place in which the political revolutionary militant is strategically rooted.

6. Alquati, "L'Università e la formazione," 96.

7. Friedrich Hölderlin, "Patmos," in *Poems of Friedrich Hölderlin*, trans. James Mitchell (San Francisco: Ithuriel's Spear, 2004), 39.

8. V. I. Lenin, *The Development of Capitalism in Russia*, in *Collected Works*, vol. 3 (Moscow: Progress Publishers, 1977), 585.

9. Lenin, *The Development of Capitalism in Russia*, 325.

10. Lenin, "What Is to Be Done?" in *Collected Works*, vol. 5 (Moscow: Progress Publishers, 1961), 509–510.

Bibliography

English Language

Alquati, Romano. "Organic Composition of Capital and Labor-Power at Olivetti" (1961). Translated by Steve Wright. *Viewpoint Magazine*, September 27, 2013. https://viewpointmag.com/2013/09/27/organic-composition-of-capital-and-labor-power-at-olivetti-1961/.

Alquati, Romano. "Struggle at Fiat" (1964). Translated by Evan Calder Williams. *Viewpoint Magazine*, September 26, 2013. https://viewpointmag.com/2013/09/26/struggle-at-fiat-1964/.

Bologna, Sergio, et al. "The Tribe of Moles." *Italy: Autonomia—Post-Political Politics* 3, no. 3 (1980): 36–61.

Curcio, Anna. "Marxist Feminism of Rupture." *Viewpoint Magazine*, January 14, 2020. https://viewpointmag.com/2020/01/14/marxist-feminism-of-rupture/.

Hölderlin, Friedrich. "Patmos." *Poems of Friedrich Hölderlin*. Translated by James Mitchell. San Francisco: Ithuriel's Spear, 2004.

James, C. L. R. *You Don't Play with Revolution: The Montréal Lectures of CLR James*. Edited by David Austin. Edinburgh: AK Press, 2009.

Marx, Karl. *Grundrisse: Foundations of Political Economy*. Translated by Martin Nicolaus. London: Penguin Books in association with New Left Review, 1993.

Musil, Robert. *The Man without Qualities*. Edited by Burton Pike. Translated by Sophie Wilkins. New York: Vintage Books, 1996.

Negri, Antonio. *Factory of Strategy: Thirty-Three Lessons on Lenin*. Translated by Arianna Bove. New York: Columbia University Press, 2014.

Negri, Antonio. "Keynes and the Capitalist Theory of the State Post-1929." In *Revolution Retrieved: Writings on Marx, Keynes, Capitalist Crisis and New Social Subjects (1967–1983)*. London: Red Notes, 1988.

Negri, Antonio. "Marx on Cycle and Crisis." In *Revolution Retrieved: Writings on Marx, Keynes, Capitalist Crisis and New Social Subjects (1967-1983)*. London: Red Notes, 1988.

Negri, Antonio. *Marx beyond Marx: Lessons on the Grundrisse*, edited by Jim Fleming. Translated by Harry Cleaver, Michael Ryan, and Maurizio Viano. New York: Autonomedia, 1991.

Tronti, Mario. *Workers and Capital*. Translated by David Broder. London: Verso, 2019.

Wright, Steve. *Storming Heaven: Class Composition and Struggle in Italian Autonomist Marxism*. Pluto Press: July 2017.

Italian Language

Agamben, Giorgio et al. *Sentimenti dell'aldiqua. Opportunismo paura cinismo nell'età del disincanto*. Rome: Theoria, 1990.

Alquati, Romano. *Camminando per realizzare un sogno comune*. Turin: Velleità alternative, 1994.

Alquati, Romano. *Cultura, Formazione, Ricerca. Industrializzazione della produzione immateriale*. Turin: Velleità alternative, 1994.

Alquati, Romano. *Dispense di Sociologia Industriale*, volume 3. Turin: Il Segnalibro editore, 1989.

Alquati, Romano. *Donna famiglia servizi nel territorio della provincia di Cremona*. Cremona: Amministrazione provincia, 1981.

Alquati, Romano. *Introduzione a un modello sulla formazione*, volume 4, part I. Turin: Il Segnalibro editore, 1992.

Alquati, Romano. *Lavoro e attività. Per un'analisi della schiavitù neomoderna*. Rome: Manifesto libri, 1997.

Alquati, Romano. *Nella società industriale d'oggi* (2001). Rome: DeriveApprodi, forthcoming.

Alquati, Romano. *Per fare conricerca*. Rome: DeriveApprodi, 2022.

Alquati, Romano. *Sacre icone*. Padua: Calusca, 1993.

Alquati, Romano. *Sul comunicare*. Turin: Il Segnalibro editore, 1993.

Alquati, Romano. *Sulla riproduzione della capacità umana vivente. L'industrializzazione della soggettività*. Rome: DeriveApprodi, 2021.

Alquati, Romano. "L'università e la formazione: L'incorporamento del sapere sociale nel lavoro vivo." *Aut aut*, no. 154 (July–August 1976).

Alquati, Romano, Nicola Negri, and Andrea Sormano. *Università di ceto medio e proletariato intellettuale*. Turin: Stampatori, 1978.

Alquati, Romano. *Sulla FIAT e altri scritti*. Milan: Feltrinelli, 1975.

Alquati, Romano, with Maurizio Pentenero and Jean-Louis Weissberg. *Sul virtuale*. Turin: Velleità alternative, 1994.

Asor Rosa, Alberto. *Le armi della critica. Scritti e saggi degli anni ruggenti (1960–1970)*. Turin: Einaudi, 2011.

Asor Rosa, Alberto. *Le due società. Ipotesi sulla crisi italiana*. Turin: Einaudi, 1977.

Bedani, Francesco, and Ioannilli, Francesca, eds. *Un cane in chiesa. Militanza, categorie e conricerca di Romano Alquati*. Rome: DeriveApprodi, 2020.

Berardi, Franco. *Quarant'anni contro il lavoro*, edited by Federico Campagna. Rome: DeriveApprodi, 2017.

Bianchini, Guido. *Sul sindacato e altri scritti*. Padua: Quaderni del Progetto, 1990.

Bianciardi, Luciano. *Il lavoro culturale*. Milan: Feltrinelli, 1957.

Bianciardi, Luciano. *La vita agra*. Milan: Rizzoli, 1962.

Bologna, Sergio. "Operaismo e composizione di classe." In *Genealogie del futuro. Sette lezioni per sovvertire il presente*, ed. Gigi Roggero and Adelino Zanini. Verona: Ombre Corte, 2013.

Bologna, Sergio, and Francesco Ciafalon. "I tecnici come produttori e come prodotto." *Quaderni piacentini*, March 1969.

Bologna, Sergio, and Giairo Daghini. *Maggio '68 in Francia*. Rome: DeriveApprodi, 2008.

Bologna, Sergio, George P. Rawick, Mauro Gobbini, Antonio Negri, Luciano Ferrari Bravo, and Ferruccio Gambino. *Operai e stato. Lotte operaie e riforma dello stato capitalistico tra rivoluzione d'Ottobre e New Deal*. Milan: Feltrinelli: 1972.

Chicchi, Federico, and Cominu, Salvatore. "Inchiesta e conricerca." In *Genealogie del futuro. Sette lezioni per sovvertire il presente*, ed. Gigi Roggero and Adelino Zanini. Verona: Ombre Corte, 2013.

di Leo, Rita. *L'esperimento profano. Dal capitalismo al socialismo e viceversa.* Rome: Ediesse, 2012.

Giovannelli, Giovanni, and Sbrogiò, Gianni. *Guido Bianchini. Ritratto di un maestro dell'operaismo.* Rome: DeriveApprodi, 2021.

Gobbi, Romolo. *Com'eri bella classe operaia. Storie, fatti e misfatti dell'operaismo italiano.* Milan: Longanesi, 1989.

Magnaghi, Alberto, ed. *"Quaderni del territorio": Dalla città fabbrica alla città digitale. Saggi e ricerche (1976–1981).* Rome: DeriveApprodi, 2021.

Marazzi, Christian. *Il comunismo del capitale. Finanziarizzazione, biopolitiche del lavoro e crisi globale.* Verona: Ombre Corte, 2010.

Marazzi, Christian. *Diario della crisi infinita.* Verona: Ombre Corte, 2015.

Meriggi, Maria Grazia. *Composizione di classe e teoria del partito. Sul marxismo degli anni '60.* Bari: Dedalo, 1978.

Negri, Antonio. *Dall'operaio massa all'operaio sociale. Intervista sull'operaismo*, edited by Paolo Pozzi and Roberta Tomassini. Milan: Multhipla edizioni, 1979.

Negri, Antonio. *Storia di un comunista.* Milan: Ponte alle Grazie, 2015.

Ritter, Gerhard A., and Susanne Miller, eds. *La rivoluzione tedesca 1918–1919. I consigli operai e il tradimento della socialdemocrazia tedesca.* Preface by Sergio Bologna. Milan: Feltrinelli, 1969.

Roggero, Gigi, Guido Borio, and Francesca Pozzi. *Futuro anteriore. Dai "Quaderni rossi" ai movimenti globali: Ricchezze e limiti dell'operaismo italiano.* Rome: DeriveApprodi, 2002.

Roggero, Gigi, Borio, Guido, and Pozzi, Francesca, eds. *Gli operaisti.* Rome: DeriveApprodi, 2005.

Roggero, Gigi, and Adelino Zanini, eds. *Genealogie del futuro. Sette lezioni per sovvertire il presente.* Verona: Ombre Corte, 2013.

Rosdolsky, Roman. *Genesi e struttura del "Capitale" di Marx.* Translated by Bruno Maffi. Rome: Laterza, 1975.

Roth, Karl Heinz. *L'altro movimento operaio. Storia della repressione capitalistica in Germania dal 1880 a oggi.* Translated by Lapo Berti. Milan: Feltrinelli, 1976.

Sacchetto, Devi, and Gianni Sbrogiò. *Quando il potere è operaio. Autonomia e soggettività politica a Porto Marghera (1960–1980).* Rome: Manifestolibri, 2009.

Scavino, Marco. *Potere operaio. La storia. La teoria*, vol. 1. Rome: DeriveApprodi, 2018.

Tagliapietra, Donato. *Gli autonomi*, vol. 5: *L'autonomia operaia vicentina. Dalla rivolta di Valdagno alla repressione di Thiene*. Rome: DeriveApprodi, 2019.

Tronti, Mario. "Introduzione." In Karl Marx, *Scritti inediti di economia politica*. Rome: Editori Riuniti, 1963.

Tronti, Mario. *Con le spalle al futuro. Per un altro dizionario politico*. Rome: Editori Riuniti, 1992.

Tronti, Mario. *Dello spirito libero. Frammenti di vita e di pensiero*. Milan: Il Saggiatore, 2015.

Tronti, Mario. *Noi operaisti*. Rome: DeriveApprodi, 2009.

Tronti, Mario. *La politica al tramonto*. Turin: Einaudi, 1998.

Tronti, Mario. "Rileggendo 'La libertà comunista.'" In Guido Liguori, *Galvano Della Volpe. Un altro marxismo*. Rome: Fahrenheit 451, 2000.

Tronti, Mario. "Tra materialismo dialettico e filosofia della prassi. Gramsci e Labriola." In *La città futura. Saggi sulla figura e il pensiero di Antonio Gramsci*, ed. Alberto Caracciolo and Giannio Scalia. Milan: Feltrinelli, 1959.

Trotta, Giuseppe, and Fabio Milana. *L'operaismo degli anni Sessanta. Da "Quaderni rossi" a "classe operaia."* Rome: DeriveApprodi, 2008.